*A Swiss-American Historical Society Publication*

# Swiss Festivals

# In

# North America

*A Resource Guide*

Donald G. Tritt, Editor

Masthof Press
Morgantown, Pennsylvania
1999

SWISS FESTIVALS IN NORTH AMERICA
A RESOURCE GUIDE

Copyright © 1999 by
Swiss-American Historical Society

*For copies and information about special purchase prices, contact the Swiss-American Historical Society, 6440 North Bosworth Avenue, Chicago, IL 60626.*

---

**ADVICE**
As event planning must be conducted far in advance, the festival dates and times given here are subject to change. Before planning a trip, it is important to verify dates and times with the contact persons designated for each festival.

---

Grateful acknowledgment is made to the following artists, authors, and publishers for permission granted:

The Society for the Promotion of Science and Scholarship, Inc., for material from "Leisure-Time Activities: Sports, Games, and Hiking," by Hans Brunner in *Modern Switzerland* (ed.) J. Murray Luck, 1978, and "Sports" by Bernard Thurnheer in *The New Switzerland* (eds.) Rolf Kieser and Kurtz R. Spillman, 1996.

Switzerland Tourism (formerly Swiss National Tourist Office) for: *Traditions and Popular Festivals in Switzerland* by Erich Schwabe, 1971.

Penguin/Putnam Press for: "Popular Fétes and Festivals," in *Swiss Life In Town and Country* by Alfred Thomas Story, 1904.

The Scarecrow Press, Inc., for: "Swiss Migration to the United States: A Historical Overview": by Leo Schelbert in *Dictionary of American Immigration History*, Francesco Cordasco (ed.), 1990. (As adapted by Leo Schelbert, 1999).

Macmillan General Reference USA, A Division of AHSUOG, Inc., for Swiss map and "Area and Population" diagram and "The Cantons of the Swiss Confederation" from Baedeker's *Switzerland*. Copyright © 1993 by Baedeker Stuttgart; and for "Discovering the Music of Switzerland," from Frommer's *Switzerland*, 7th ed. Copyright © 1995 by Simon & Schuster, Inc.

Hermann Schelbert for bookcover artwork.
Ursula Kaeshammer Alther for scherenschnitt artwork.

Library of Congress Number: 99-70547
International Standard Book Number: 1-883294-87-8

*All rights reserved.*

*Printed 1999 by*
Masthof Press
220 Mill Road
Morgantown, PA 19543-9701

# Dedication

Dedicated to the memory of the many
Swiss immigrants
who undertook the challenge of
making the "New World" their home.

In addition, I wish to dedicate this book to the
memory of my immigrant grandparents,
JOSEPH GUSTAV TRITT,
whose ancestry originated in the
Obersimmental, Canton Bern, Switzerland
and
VERENA SCHUDEL,
whose ancestry originated in
Beggingen, Canton Schaffhausen, Switzerland

# Contents

*Dedication* . . . . . . . . . . . . . . . . . . . . . . . . . . . . . . . . . . . . . . . iii
*Acknowledgments* . . . . . . . . . . . . . . . . . . . . . . . . . . . . . . . . . vi
*Introduction* . . . . . . . . . . . . . . . . . . . . . . . . . . . . . . . . . . . . . vii

Swiss Migration To The United States:
   A Historical Overview . . . . . . . . . . . . . . . . . . . . . . . . . 1

Popular Fêtes And Festivals . . . . . . . . . . . . . . . . . . . . . . . . 9

Traditions And Popular Festivals In Switzerland . . . . . . . . . 21

Sports, Games, And Recreation . . . . . . . . . . . . . . . . . . . . . 60

Discovering The Music Of Switzerland . . . . . . . . . . . . . . . 68

Scherenschnitt . . . . . . . . . . . . . . . . . . . . . . . . . . . . . . . . . . 70

The Flag Of Switzerland . . . . . . . . . . . . . . . . . . . . . . . . . . 73

Map Of Switzerland . . . . . . . . . . . . . . . . . . . . . . . . . . . . . 74

The Cantons Of The Swiss Confederation . . . . . . . . . . . . . 75

North American Swiss Festivals . . . . . . . . . . . . . . . . . . . . 76
   Alberta . . . . . . . . . . . . . . . . . . . . . . . . . . . . . . . . . . . . 76
   British Columbia . . . . . . . . . . . . . . . . . . . . . . . . . . . . 78
   Ontario . . . . . . . . . . . . . . . . . . . . . . . . . . . . . . . . . . . 80
   California . . . . . . . . . . . . . . . . . . . . . . . . . . . . . . . . . 83
   Colorado . . . . . . . . . . . . . . . . . . . . . . . . . . . . . . . . . 93
   Illinois . . . . . . . . . . . . . . . . . . . . . . . . . . . . . . . . . . . 96
   Indiana . . . . . . . . . . . . . . . . . . . . . . . . . . . . . . . . . . 100

  Maryland . . . . . . . . . . . . . . . . . . . . . . . . . . . . . . 105
  Minnesota . . . . . . . . . . . . . . . . . . . . . . . . . . . . . 106
  New Jersey . . . . . . . . . . . . . . . . . . . . . . . . . . . . 111
  New York . . . . . . . . . . . . . . . . . . . . . . . . . . . . . 112
  Ohio . . . . . . . . . . . . . . . . . . . . . . . . . . . . . . . . . . 118
  Oregon . . . . . . . . . . . . . . . . . . . . . . . . . . . . . . . 123
  South Carolina . . . . . . . . . . . . . . . . . . . . . . . . . 127
  Tennessee . . . . . . . . . . . . . . . . . . . . . . . . . . . . . 128
  Utah . . . . . . . . . . . . . . . . . . . . . . . . . . . . . . . . . 129
  Washington . . . . . . . . . . . . . . . . . . . . . . . . . . . 133
  West Virginia . . . . . . . . . . . . . . . . . . . . . . . . . . 135
  Wisconsin . . . . . . . . . . . . . . . . . . . . . . . . . . . . . 141

English Language Bibliography . . . . . . . . . . . . . . . . . . 160
  A. Swiss Folk Traditions . . . . . . . . . . . . . . . . . . 160
  B. Swiss Immigration And Swiss Settlements
    In North America . . . . . . . . . . . . . . . . . . . . 161
  C. Swiss Genealogical Research . . . . . . . . . . . . 172
  D. Swiss Cookbooks . . . . . . . . . . . . . . . . . . . . 173

Swiss Consular Representation In North America . . . . . . . . 175

Switzerland Tourism Offices In North America . . . . . . . . . . 178

Swiss-American Historical Society and
  Membership Application . . . . . . . . . . . . . . . . . . 180

Tell Us! What Have We Forgotten? . . . . . . . . . . . . . . . . . 182

Publications Order Form . . . . . . . . . . . . . . . . . . . . . . . . 183

*Index To Events By Month* . . . . . . . . . . . . . . . . . . . . . 185
*Advertisements* . . . . . . . . . . . . . . . . . . . . . . . . . . . . . 189
*About The Author* . . . . . . . . . . . . . . . . . . . . . . . . . . . 197

# Acknowledgments

A work of this kind requires the support and cooperation of many persons. The idea for this book was proposed by the author at the 1992 annual meeting of the Swiss-American Historical Society, and strongly supported by Erdmann Schmocker, President of the Society, and Leo Schelbert, Editor of the Society's publications.

In addition, I am grateful for the support of the members of the Society and for the contributions of the various Swiss festival coordinators across Canada and the United States for without their submissions, this book could not have been compiled.

# INTRODUCTION

One purpose of the Swiss-American Historical Society is to unite people interested in the involvement of Swiss and their descendants in American life and in all aspects of Swiss-American relations. In addressing this goal, members of the Society have observed that Swiss descendants are expressing an increased interest in cultural, historical, and musical events linked to their Swiss heritage. Discussion of this phenomenon resulted in the idea that a directory of Swiss festivals in North America could be one way to respond not only to the interests of second- and third-generation Swiss descendants, but also to native-born Swiss.

Members of the Society felt that issuing such a directory could be one way to fulfill several important goals:

- to publicize regularly-occurring events in North America which celebrate Swiss heritage;

- to increase and enhance the visiblity of Swiss in North America;

- to give Swiss-born and current-day Swiss descendants a cultural and historical link to Switzerland;

- to assist in making placements for visiting artists, musicians, and scholars from Switzerland;

- to make available to interested persons books, articles, and other materials, in English, which present the history and meaning of Swiss festivals, folkways, legends, and traditions.

A modest predecessor of the current book was issued in 1995 and was published in-house by the Society. This initial work contained descriptions of thirty-nine festivals occurring in sixteen different states. To present festival information for the current book, a letter of inquiry, accompanied by a questionnaire, was sent to presidents of 300 Swiss clubs and organizations in the United States and 60 in Canada. From this mailing, responses were received describing the 52 festivals contained here.

For inclusion in this directory, the following criteria were used:

1) the festival or event has as its central purpose the celebration of Swiss heritage and culture;
2) the festival or event is offered on a regular recurring basis;
3) the festival or event is open to the public.

This book will be useful for Swiss festival organizations, attendees at the various festivals, and Swiss communities and clubs in North America. In addition, it can help in the planning of leisure touring groups in the United States and Canada, and facilitate the placement of tourist, artistic, musical, and scholarly visits from Switzerland. Further, travel magazines and journals as well as the general public may make use of this book. In all, we expect this book will significantly enhance the Swiss presence in North America and increase the number of persons participating in the various festivals.

Drawing from the response received from the earlier edition of this book, we realized that such a work as this could serve as a guide to resources other communities might utilize to create Festivals of Swiss Heritage. With this in mind, we have added major new sections to this current edition.

Similar to festivals celebrated in Switzerland, some of the festivals described here offer a single-focused activity, while others offer a wide range of Swiss events. Most of the festivals described here have come about because of the hard work of dedicated volunteers eager to perpetuate Swiss culture and traditions. The festivals range from local events attended by a few to festivals so organized and so well-known that they draw patrons from far and wide.

We are hopeful that this book will increase awareness of the role of the Swiss-American Historical Society in preserving and fostering the celebration of Swiss culture in America. To participate in this work, we earnestly invite your membership in the Society. Founded in 1927, the Society promotes an active program of research, scholarly forums, and publication in all aspects of Swiss-American relations. Members receive three newsletters per year, copies of books published with the help of the Society, and occasionally reprints of pertinent articles. The Society holds its annual meetings in October and organizes occasional regional meetings. All work of the Society is done on a volunteer basis. Further information about the Swiss-American Historical Society and a membership form is given at the end of this book.

We hope you enjoy this edition of *Swiss Festivals In North America: A Resource Guide*. Please write with your comments and suggestions.

                                      Donald G. Tritt
                                      81 Donald Ross Drive
                                      Granville, OH 43023-9794
                                      Telephone: (740) 587-0213

# Swiss Migration to the United States:

## A Historical Overview[1]

*by Leo Schelbert*

Although about half a million people are estimated to have left Switzerland since 1600 to reside at least for some time in what is now the territory of the United States, the involvement of Swiss in American history and life is little known. Their relative invisibility derives from their being viewed as either German, French, or Italian, depending on whether their native tongue in Switzerland was German, French, Italian, or Romansh. Between 1700 and 1820 about fifty thousand Swiss arrived in North America; between 1820 and 1930 some 265,000 are estimated to have arrived in the United States. After the Great Depression and World War Two, when migrations resumed if on a smaller scale, the Swiss presence remained fairly steady. In 1980 it was composed of 235,355 Swiss Americans of single and 746,188 of multiple, that is also of Swiss ancestry. In 1989 Swiss who were registered at the various consular offices of the United States numbered 55,980, in 1996 63,996; of the latter 21,477 had exclusively Swiss, 42,519 also American citizenship.

### Swiss at Home and Abroad

These Swiss were part of a much larger migratory movement. In the sixteenth century some 50,000 to 100,000 Swiss served abroad as soldiers or craftsmen; in the seventeenth century 250,000 to 300,000, and in the eighteenth century about 350,000 did so. At the same time foreign-born entered Switzerland. For the years 1798 to 1914 the demographer W. Bickel offers the following estimates: From 1798 to 1850 about 50,000

---

[1] This is an updated and revised version of "Swiss Migration to the United States: A Historical Overview" by Leo Schelbert in *Dictionary of American Immigration History*, edited by Francesco Cordasco (Metuchen, N.J.: Scarecrow Press, 1990): 698-703; reprinted by permission.

foreign-born entered Switzerland whereas about 100,000 Swiss went abroad; from 1850 to 1914 some 410,000 Swiss left home and 409,000 foreign-born resided in Switzerland who hailed mainly from neighboring countries. In 1880, for instance, of the 211,000 foreign-born in Switzerland 45.1 percent came from Germany, 27.8 from France, and 19.5 from Italy. Of the 234,000 Swiss abroad in 1880, 38 percent resided in the United States, 29 percent in France, 13 percent in Germany, 5 percent each in Italy and Argentina, and small contingents of Swiss were to be found in nearly every corner of the globe.

Why did Swiss migrate? Two contexts must be distinguished. On the *personal* level social forces such as strife between spouses, parents and children, in-laws, neighbors, or villagers predominated. Some sought quick riches in the expectation of speedy return; others hoped to hold on to their accustomed craft in lands abroad or hoped for expanded opportunities in the wider world. Careers in commerce, the military, or the missions attracted others. On the *systemic* level, entrenched migratory traditions, participation in the expansion of Europeans and their descendants into territories overseas, and transnational networks of economic activity provided the most important contexts.

## SWISS IN BRITISH NORTH AMERICA

The first known Swiss to have set foot on North American soil was the Bernese Diebold von Erlach (1541-1565), member of a French Huguenot expedition attempting to gain a permanent foothold on the southern North American coast. He perished in the ensuing conflict with the Spaniards who founded St. Augustine, Florida, as a protective measure in 1665. In 1607 some "Switzers" served as craftsmen in Jamestown where a William Henry Volday [Walder ?] incurred the wrath of Captain John Smith (1579-1631), the early English leader of the colony. In 1687 the French Swiss Jean François Gignilliat of Vevey, the ancestor of a large southern family, received some 3,000 acres from the South Carolina proprietors "to encourage more of the Swisse nation" to settle there. Some Swiss were also among the settlers of Germantown which was founded by German Quaker-Mennonites in 1683. Around 1700 Franz Louis Michel, an enterprising Swiss from the city of Bern searched Maryland and Pennsylvania for mines and a suitable place for a large Swiss settlement.

In 1710 Christoph von Graffenried (1661-1743) from Yverdon, Canton Bern, hoped to regain lost wealth by leading a group of Swiss and

Palatines to North Carolina. They were part of the 1709 exodus of some 13,000 people who planned to settle in British domains in response to Queen Anne's widely advertised liberal immigration policies. At the confluence of the Neuse and Trent rivers Graffenried founded New Bern, but returned home in 1713. His grandson Tscharner, however, born in 1691 in Virginia, became the progenitor of a large southern family.

In the 1690s the religious movement known as Pietism brought dissension to the Swiss churches of the Reformed persuasion. Several ministers lost their posts, among them Samuel Güldin (1664-1745), who went in 1710 to Pennsylvania. In the same year a first group of Swiss (Mennonite) Brethren and Sisters settled at Conestoga along the Pequea Creek where they bought a tract of some 10,000 acres. During the next four decades some 4,000 Swiss Brethren and Sisters followed and moved southward and westward. They lived on individual farms and formed congregations of some twenty to thirty families. Their religiously based way of life preserved many features of their Swiss and Palatine origin.

Also several thousand Swiss Reformed moved to Pennsylvania, Virginia, and the Carolinas. They were joined by several ministers among whom Michael Schlatter (1716-1790) was the most prominent. In the 1730s Jean Pierre Purry (1675-1736) of Neuchâtel conducted an effective emigration campaign and founded Purryburg some twenty miles upriver from Savannah, Georgia. He brought some 450 people to South Carolina and induced about as many to move to other areas of the North American coast.

Many Swiss settled as craftsmen or business people in cities like Philadelphia and Charleston. Noteworthy among them are Jeremiah Theus (1719-1774), a successful portrait painter in Charleston, and Johann Joachim Züblin (1724-1781), a Swiss Reformed preacher from St. Gallen, who as John J. Zubly was actively involved in the revolutionary agitation but opposed independence. Henri Bouquet (1725-1791); the brothers Jacques (1725-1776), Augustin (1723-1786), and Marc (1736-1781) Prévost; and Frédéric Haldimand (1725-1791) were high-ranking officers in the British colonial forces opposing the revolutionary army.

During the revolutionary crisis Swiss immigrants and their descendants followed the general pattern. Some remained loyal to the British Crown, others stayed aloof, and still others fought with the rebel forces. The Reformed minister Abraham Blumer (1736-1822), for instance, supported the Revolution. Michael Schlatter first joined the British forces, but when he realized that his sons fought on the rebel side, he refused to remain in the military. John J. Zubly, in contrast, although he had been severely critical of British policies, remained loyal to the Crown, was tried in Georgia, and lost a good part of his property. Although the initial immigrants differed quite widely in their response to the new land, their descendants blended easily into colonial culture and, the Mennonites excepted, became indistinguishable from the general population.

After the 1750s, Swiss group immigration had largely ceased, but single families or individuals arrived steadily throughout the next decades. In 1780 the Genevan Albert Gallatin (1761-1849) arrived in Maine, then briefly taught French at Harvard, and finally settled in Pennsylvania. He actively participated in politics and from 1801 to 1812 served as secretary of the treasury in the Jefferson and Madison administrations. He also distinguished himself as a diplomat, scholar and was co-founder of New York University.

## SWISS IN THE UNITED STATES, 1820 TO 1930

During the nineteenth century the United States transformed itself by conquest from an Atlantic coastal nation to one of continental size. The conquered territories were cleared of the indigenous peoples and resettled by descendants of the colonial population, to a smaller degree also by people from abroad. The Swiss participated in that migratory movement. Between 1820 and 1890 over 200,000 arrived in the expanding United States. Most Swiss going abroad, however, went to European countries. In 1850, for instance, 63.4 percent of the 72,500 Swiss abroad resided in countries of Europe, 28 percent had moved to nations in the Americas, the rest to other parts of the world. In 1880, the proportion of the 234,000 Swiss abroad shifted to 51.1 percent for Europe and 46.1 for the Americas; in 1928 the proportion moved back to 72.9 and 23.9 percent, respectively.

The majority of Swiss dispersed widely in the newly opened areas for white settlement or went to the rapidly growing urban centers. Yet a series of initially quite homogeneous Swiss settlements did emerge. One of the first was Vevay, Indiana, on the Ohio; it was founded in 1803 by Jean Jacques Dufour (1767-1827) who had decided in his youth to introduce viticulture into the United States. Although success was moderate, by 1810 the settlement produced some 2,400 gallons of wine that "connoisseurs thought to be better than the claret of Bordeaux." In 1831 members of the Köpfli and Suppiger families established Highland,

Illinois, some sixty miles east of St. Louis on the Looking Glass Prairie. By 1870 some 1,500 Swiss had settled in the region, among them the Bandelier family. Adolph Bandelier (1840-1914) became a leading anthropologist of the Southwest whose works are still valued today. Wisconsin attracted some 8,000 Swiss. They centered in Sauk County; in Alma, Buffalo County; and in Green County, especially Monroe and New Glarus. In 1845, 119 Swiss arrived from the Glarus Valley of Switzerland to found a New Glarus. By 1860 the inhabitants cultivated over 10,000 acres, had established 149 farms, and numbered 960 people. In the 1870s dairying replaced wheat growing. In the mid-twentieth century New Glarus became increasingly conscious of its roots. An "Historical Village" and festivals celebrating Wilhelm Tell and Heidi yearly attract numerous visitors to the area.

After 1817 descendants of Swiss Mennonites moved westward into the midwestern territories, joined by coreligionists directly from Switzerland. Predominantly Swiss foundations were Sonnenberg (1817) and Chippewa (1825) in Ohio, Berne (1838) in Indiana, and Madison Township (1849) in Iowa. In the second half of the nineteenth century the movement continued into the farmlands of Missouri, Kansas, and Oregon; the main settlements were Whitewater (1883) in Butler County, Kansas; Tipton (1886) in Morgan and Moniteau Counties, Missouri; and Silverton and Salem in Oregon. Like their eighteenth century counterparts, these settlements were not compact villages, but consisted of family farms forming Swiss Mennonite congregations. The impact of the American environment transformed several of them; English replaced German, a trained clergy the lay ministry, and town living the farming way of life on individual homesteads.

In the 1880s a "reveil"—that is an awakening—occurred among the Reformed churches of French-speaking Switzerland. Some of the awakened became "Open" or "Plymouth Brethren," and several families moved to the environs of Knoxville, Tennessee, where they continued to practice their evangelical faith for some generations.

Several secular Swiss settlements emerged in the second half of the nineteenth century. Tell City on the Ohio in southern Indiana was started in 1857 as a business venture. In the later 1860s West Virginia actively recruited European immigrants to settle its mountainous regions. In 1869 Helvetia was founded, followed by Alpena, West Huttonsville, Cotton Hill, Kendalia, and New St. Gallen. Also in 1869 Peter Staub (1827-1904) founded Grütli in Grundy County, Tennessee; by 1886 the settlement counted 330 Swiss among its 400 inhabitants. In 1881 two Swiss entrepreneurs promoted the founding of Bernstadt, Kentucky; by the end of the decade over a thousand Swiss had settled in the region that included also East Bernstadt, Grünheim, and Crab Orchard in Lincoln County.

In 1839 Johann August Sutter (1803-1880) established a vast plantation called Helvetia on California's Mexican frontier. The discovery of gold on his property in 1849 attracted some 300,000 people from all over the world to California who hoped for quick riches in the exploration of gold mines. Two-thirds of Sutter's land claims were declared invalid by the United States government, which had annexed the West Coast to its own domain after the 1847 war against Mexico. After 1850 California also attracted many Italian Swiss, mostly single men in search of work who returned home after some years. By the end of the century, however, family migration predominated and the majority became permanent immigrants engaged in grape growing, dairying, and cattle raising. They concentrated in the coastal region of Marin County and in the Central Valley's Stanislaus County. Others settled in cities like San Francisco and Sacramento.

In the second half of the nineteenth century the Mormon mission induced about a thousand Swiss to settle in Utah; they centered in Midway, Wasatch County; Santa Clara, Washington County; Providence, Cache County; and in Bern and Geneva in Bear Lake County, Idaho. These immigrants had large families, especially during the phase of plural marriages, and their descendants took an active part in building up and recruiting further compatriots for their New Zion.

The immigration of Swiss Catholics led to the founding of monasteries and convents. In 1852 the Benedictine monastery of Einsiedeln, Switzerland, founded St. Meinrad, Indiana, which developed into an educational and pastoral center for German-speaking Catholics who settled in that region. It also became the nucleus of the Swiss Benedictine, today called Pan-Benedictine, congregation. The Swiss Benedictine monastery of Engelberg supported the founding of Conception, Missouri, and of Mount Angel in Oregon. From these foundations further monasteries were established. Benedictine sisters followed the example of the monks; Anselma Felber (1843-1883) founded the convent at Conception, Missouri, which later moved to Clyde as the Benedictine Convent of the Perpetual Adoration; Gertrud Leupi (1825-1904), from the same Swiss Benedictine Convent of Maria Rickenbach, Canton Nidwalden, founded a convent in Maryville which then was moved to Yankton, South Dakota. Franz von

Sales Brunner (1795-1859) introduced the Order of the Precious Blood into Ohio, and a first Capuchin Friary was founded in Milwaukee in 1859.

A good number of Swiss immigrants moved to urban centers. In 1870, for instance, 2,902 Swiss lived in St. Louis, Missouri; 2,844 in New York City; and 1,791 in Philadelphia. In 1890 New York counted 6,355 Swiss, Chicago 2,262, St. Louis 2,209, and San Francisco 1,696. Other concentrations of urban Swiss were in Paterson, New Jersey; Cleveland, Ohio; Pittsburgh, Pennsylvania; Portland, Oregon; and Milwaukee, Wisconsin. In these centers Swiss immigrants created a variety of organizations that were largely adaptations of institutions from their home country. Before the Civil War, for instance, the New York City Swiss had a Benevolent Society, a Helvetia Rifle Club, a Society for the Benefit of the Sick, a Helvetia Lodge, and a Helvetia Men's Choir. These were designed to assist those in need, to create social cohesion, and to preserve Swiss traditions. In the second half of the nineteenth century the North American Grütli-Bund, which in 1915 counted six thousand members, strove for Swiss-American unity on the national level. The democratic and culturally pluralist orientation of the Swiss made them easily blend into mainstream American society where they did not meet obstacles that derived from their ethnicity.

Some nineteenth-century Swiss achieved national renown. Among them were Louis Agassiz (1807-1873), a natural scientist noted for his anti-Darwinian stand; the Guggenheims of Philadelphia, who had come from Lengnau, Canton Argau, in 1847; Martin Henni (1805-1881) who became the first Catholic archbishop of Milwaukee, and Philip Schaff (1819-1893), after 1870 a leading ecumenical Protestant theologian.

## SWISS IN THE UNITED STATES SINCE 1920

By 1920 the United States had reached its present territorial size and had joined the world powers. Immigration became regulated by the quota system, set for Swiss at 3,752 per year in 1921, and by 1929 reduced to 1,707. The new arrivals were mainly professionals, often connected with large international firms such as Nestlé, Ciba-Geigy, and Holderbank. With the advent of air travel these newcomers cross the Atlantic often, and many do not settle permanently in the United States. They are the counterpart of Americans in Switzerland.

Many twentieth-century Swiss had remarkable careers in the United States. Among them are Othmar Ammann (1879-1965), the designer and builder of famous suspension bridges in the environs of New York City; William Lescaze (1896-1969), a designer of early skyscrapers; Adolph Meyer (1866-1950), who dominated American psychiatry up to 1940; Ernest Bloch (1880-1957), the creator of modern liturgical Jewish music; Mary Sandoz (1901-1966), a noted novelist and historian; and William Wyler (1902-1981), a producer of acclaimed films and documentaries.

Today the Swiss-American group is composed of four major strands. First, the descendants of eighteenth-century Swiss immigrants have, if at all, mainly a genealogical interest in their origin. Second, descendants of Swiss Anabaptist groups, that is, about two-thirds of all American Mennonites, view their ancestors as formulators and prototypes of their persuasions who lived their faith under adverse Swiss conditions. The third group, the offspring of nineteenth- and twentieth-century immigrants, are often fully assimilated already in the second generation, but preserve ties with their country of origin by frequent visits and by active participation in Swiss-American societies. A fourth group consists of recent newcomers who adhere to an updated version of Swissness and are often active in strengthening the bonds of Swiss Americans with their past.

## REFERENCES

Swiss American Historical Society, ed., *Prominent Americans of Swiss Origin* (1932); John Paul von Grüningen, ed., *The Swiss in the United States* (1940); Delbert L. Gratz, *Bernese Anabaptists and Their American Descendants* (1953); Leo Schelbert, "On Becoming an Emigrant: A Structural View of Eighteenth and Nineteenth Century Swiss Data," *Perspectives in American History* 7 (1973): 440-495; Leo Schelbert, "Swiss," in *Harvard Encyclopedia of American Ethnic Groups* (1980): 981-987; Giorgio Cheda, *L'emigrazione ticinese in California* (1981), two of five projected volumes; James P. Allen and Eugene J. Turner, eds., *We the People. An Atlas of America's Ethnic Diversity* (Macmillan 1988), 56-58; Leo Schelbert, "Swiss Americans," in *Gale Encyclopedia of Multi-Cultural America*, vol. 2 (1995): 1298-1308. Urspeter Schelbert, ed. and comp., *Swiss Colonists in 19th Century America.* [Facsimile edition of Adelrich Steinach, *Geschichte und Leben der Schweizer Kolonien,* 1889], with Index, pp. 393-525; Urspeter Schelbert, "Index" [of 33 years of the journal], *SAHS [Swiss American Historical Society] Review* 33, No. 3 (November 1997): 1-114, published by Masthof Press, 1998.

# Popular Fêtes and Festivals[1]

*by Alfred Thomas Story*

The Swiss throw the same zeal into their popular *fêtes* and rejoicings which they throw into almost everything else they take in hand. It is rare that they can be charged with entering into any enterprise, be it of work or play, in a half-hearted manner. Thus far the virus of ennui and its sequent cynicism, which are so apt to attack and to enervate great and successful nations, have not touched the Swiss people. They are yet, as it were, in their buoyant youth, with the man's task still before them; and whenever there is an undertaking which appeals to the national heart, they apply themselves to it with all the abundant energy of youthful days. In nothing is this spirit so strikingly shown as in connection with some of the popular *fêtes* and gatherings that break the monotony of the revolving year.

These celebrations, if added together, form a host. They are, however, of two kinds—first, national, in the sense of uniting the suffrages of the whole people, and, second, cantonal. Cantonal *fêtes* are generally of a semi-religious character, as celebrating some supreme event in the history of the canton—a battle, the winning of independence, an evidence of Divine mercy, or what not. Of such is the annual feast that takes place in the canton of Geneva on the first of June, in commemoration of its union with the Swiss Confederation. It is held religiously as a general holiday, and the day is always opened with service in the churches.

Another celebration of the kind is that of Näfels in the little canton of Glarus, which is held on the first Thursday in April, that being the anniversary of the battle fought there against the Austrians in 1388. On the ninth of April in that year, some six hundred men of Glarus encountered a force of between five and six thousand Austrians, and utterly defeating them, preserved the independence of the canton. In

---

[1] Reprinted by permission of Penguin/Putnam from *Swiss Life in Town and Country* by Alfred Thomas Story, 1904, 221-242.

remembrance whereof the Glarner, peasant and workman alike, makes his way on the day in question to Näfels, and listens, under the open sky, to a sermon tuned to the occasion, and after returning thanks to God for His great mercy then and since, grasps his *Fahrstecken* with a tighter grip, and goes homeward again. Many other celebrations of a similar nature are to be met with in various parts of Switzerland, simple, heartfelt affairs for the most part, extremely local in character, and highly characteristic.

Very different are the more general, and more truly national, *fêtes* and assemblages that mark the festive season. Of these, the most noteworthy is the annual shooting-match, the *Tir Fédéral,* as it is called in French. This is held at a different place every year, most towns of any importance in the Confederation having been the scene of the *Fest* at one time or another, some of them more than once. This movable nature of the gathering tends to give spirit to its annual recurrence, each town vying with its predecessor in the heartiness of its welcome to competitors and visitors and in the splendour of its preparations.

These shooting-matches are of very ancient date, and can be traced back to the fourteenth century, when Zaehringen had a society for the encouragement of shooting, and Soleure had a *Tir aux fleurs*. In the course of time, however, these and other societies of the kind fell into decay, and it was only after the effects of the French Revolution had begun to crumble away that the memory of the old-time shooting-matches began to revive. The improvement in firearms tended to strengthen the reawakening, and while active-minded Swiss citizens were busy in other directions, establishing their societies for the study of natural science and for matters of public utility, others, whose thoughts turned to national defense, were launching the Swiss Society of Carabineers. The first Federal *Tir* soon followed, and since that time (1824) the festival has grown yearly in strength and importance.

It was pointed out in the early days how important these gatherings were, not merely for the purpose of improvement in shooting, but for encouraging a love of the beautiful. There is no reason why the two things should not be cultivated at one and the same time, and they have, as a matter of fact, been so cultivated, though it may be with varying degrees of success. Another aim which, it was seen, might be furthered by means of these national gatherings was that of breaking down the spirit of local patriotism—that *Kantönligeist*, as it has been so well called—which for so long stood, and still to some extent stands, in the way of a broader and more general progress. That they were turned to good account in this respect may be seen from the fact that it was at one of these annual gatherings that Dr. Zidler, of Zug, started the movement which led to the constitutional revision of 1848. Other movements of equal importance for the welfare of the country have had their initiation at the banquets of these *Schützenfest*, among others—if the popular memory may be trusted— that which led to the suppression of the Order of Jesuits in Switzerland.

It is well to remember these things, as showing that, notwithstanding that the spirit of these *fêtes* is in the main festive, underneath that spirit of gladness and rejoicing lies a very serious intention and endeavor. Although the competitors and visitors assemble at the place of meeting determined to enjoy the scenery of the district, the beautiful weather, and the open-air life, yet they never forget that, before all, they are met as Swiss citizens. Hence, when there are urgent public questions to the front, the sport side of the *Schützenfest* is apt to be lost sight of in the heat and urgency of political discussion. For your Schweizer, workman, merchant, or whatever he may be, is first and foremost a politician. He is rarely loth to enjoy "a good time," but he does not forget that he is one of the supports of the State, and that if he neglects his duty the country may neglect him.

If the *Schützenfeste* had a modest beginning, they have grown and strengthened with the years. During the closing years of the century just past, the prizes reached a total of between two and three hundred thousand francs, and the number of cartridges spent in front of the various targets amounted to an average of a million and a half, and I believe at last year's gathering this number was exceeded.

The Society of Carabineers numbered at the end of the century 1348 sections, with a membership of between sixty and seventy thousand. Its invested funds amount to 146,000 francs, and since 1899 it has subsidized the cantonal sections with a view to encourage and stimulate the practice of rifle-shooting and good-fellowship, believing that in so doing it is advancing the interests not only of the Confederation as a whole, but of each individual citizen.

Next in importance after the Federal rifle-meeting, which is held in June, come the periodical gatherings or tournaments in connection with the various gymnastic societies existing through the country, and the different clubs and associations for the encouragement of national sports of all kinds. These assemblies, in what may be termed their national aspect, date from the year 1805, when on one of the few bright days of that rainy year an *Ælplerfest*, or feast of shepherds, was held near the ruins of the Castle of Unspunnen, facing the chain of the Jungfrau and its neighboring peaks. It was simply the antique *fête* of the mountain people enlarged to admit of the participation of other cantons, which were cordially invited. Brilliant was the gathering of spectators, some from the far outland, to witness this unique display, and great was the emotion roused, especially among the Swiss themselves, when at a given signal the procession of singers, players on the Alpine horn, wrestlers, and throwers of the stone made their way into the arena around which the spectators were gathered, amid songs of welcome and the moving notes of the alphorn, which, echoed and re-echoed by the surrounding heights, stirred the hearts of the native-born to their profoundest depths.

The Bernese wrestlers, famed from of old for this sort of thing, bore off the palm from all comers; but it was to a sturdy Appenzeller that fell the prize for casting or putting the stone. Other games followed, and then, as the evening fell, all joined in the dance, under the shade of the century-old walnut trees, to the sound of the hackbrett and the violin.

When, three years later, there was a repetition of these games, six thousand spectators assembled on the classic ground of Unspunnen. Madame de Staël was among the number, and it is said that the procession of old Swiss notables, founders of their country's liberties, made a very deep impression upon her, as is noted in her work on Germany.

Down to a very recent date the *Ælplerfeste,* or gatherings of mountain shepherds and herdsmen for the purposes of sport, were the only *fêtes* characteristically national held by the Swiss, and of all the games practiced thereat that of wrestling is the most ancient. Everywhere throughout the Alps the art is cultivated by young and old alike; but in no district is it brought to such perfection as in the Bernese Oberland, the Emmenthal, and the vale of Entlebuch. The men of the last-named valley in especial are celebrated for their prowess in wrestling, having no superiors in any part of Switzerland. It is a sight to see them on the occasion of one of their periodical *Schwingfeste*, as they are called, of which three or four are generally held in the summer months, the chief of them falling on the first Sunday in September, when the stout men of Entebuch pit their strength against whoever comes, and generally manage to hold their own. The Emmenthalers, a particularly sturdy race of men, run them very close, but hitherto have been bound to acknowledge the precedence of their neighbours.

The Swiss method of wrestling is very different from the English. The competitors strip to their shirts and hose. The latter are of twill, and are made of double and even treble thickness at the waist and knees. The right hand of each wrestler grasps the waistband and the left the kneeband of his adversary. The head of each looks over the other's shoulder, while the legs are kept well apart, and the left as far back as possible. The aim of each is to lift his antagonist and get him with his back on the ground. There are many different methods of attack, and of course as many parries.

One of the special features of these *Ælplerfeste* is the procession known as the "departure for the Alps," in which everything connected with the annual start for the mountain pastures is gone through as though it were the actual thing. But in addition various games are played, including that of casting the stone, wrestling, etc.

Nothing seems to please the great body of the Swiss people so much as to see a good wrestling match. I refer, of course, to the great mass of those whose labor is mainly with their thews and sinews, and who therefore know the value of endurance and physique. A meeting of the kind, such as takes place on the Ramparts at Berne every Easter Monday, is sure to attract a concourse of spectators. These particular gatherings are famous, and bring together some of the stoutest wrestlers of the Bernese Oberland, of the Emmenthal, as well as of Lucerne and the Unterwaldens. But other cantons also have similar athletic displays. A grand festival of the kind took place at Zurich in 1894, when a Federation of Swiss Wrestlers was formed, with the object, amongst other things, of preserving the national games. The last *fête* of the Federation took place at Berne last year, when, in view of the patriotic aims of those concerned, a particularly interesting gathering took place. The intention is to revive in all its glory the old-time *Ælplerfest*, or feast of the mountains. It may be doubted whether they can do that, any more than we can revive the old village-green and maypole time. All the same, it may aid in the work of cementing the Swiss people more thoroughly together as one nation—the great aim now of Federal politicians—to revive and encourage such games and sports as casting the stone, playing the alphorn, "jodeling," joining in native dances, ballets, and other rustic pastimes, such, for instance, as the Swiss form of rackets, known as *Hornus*, the play with flags, etc.

Very popular, too, are the gymnastic clubs and societies, which, like our cricket and football clubs, lead to a good deal of intercourse between districts and cantons, to many popular gatherings of one kind or another, and every three years to a grand national *fête*. These gymnastic gatherings date back to the time of Ludwig Jahn, the "father of gymnastics," who, by his enthusiasm for physical culture, did so much for the physical development of German youth. The idea was taken up with zest by the students of the Universities of Zurich, Berne, and Basel, and while timorous politicians regarded their meetings as nothing better than schools of savagery, revolution, and immorality, they were in reality doing a patriotic work for the common country.

It was not long before gymnastic societies sprang up that were not connected with the universities, and, the idea spreading, there was a Federal *fête*. It was thought that, while the Swiss youth were thus strengthening their bodies for the well-being of themselves and their country, they would be drawn together more closely in the bonds of patriotism. For, said the moving spirits and patrons of these *fêtes*, there is nothing like doing things together in order to learn to think in common. This idea was soon developed in another form. It was soon perceived that these gymnastic societies might be made a splendid means for military education, and simple gymnastic exercises branched out into warlike games.

At first there were national *fêtes* every year, first one city or town being the scene of the function, and then another. Then the popular meeting was held every other year, and finally, since 1888, every three years. But what the gatherings thus lose as regards frequency they gain in brilliance and strength. They now stand out as among the most interesting and the most popular of Swiss *fêtes*. They are, in especial, the *fêtes* of youth, of abounding life, of enthusiasm. It is long since gymnastics were the exclusive appanage of the universities. In all the great centres of industrial life such societies have done much to improve the physique and, consequently, the general health of the workers. At the last meeting but one, held in 1897, at Schaffhausen, there were 5736 competitors, of whom over 700 took part in individual contests. Two hundred societies took part in sectional contests, while over 300, including foreign societies, were represented at the *fête*. These figures were considerably exceeded at the next triennial gathering, held at Chaux-de-Fonds in 1900. At that time the Federal Society of Gymnastics numbered 539 sections, with a membership of close upon 40,000.

One of the most striking features of later gatherings have been the exercises in groups. At Geneva, in 1891, they were the "hit" of the *fête*.

At Lugano, three years later, some three thousand gymnasts assisted at similar evolutions, and may be said with truth to have caused a sensation. Everything helped thereto—the place of meeting, with its century-old trees casting a grateful shade, the surrounding hills, built as of emerald and amethyst, and the overarching vault of heaven without a fleck on its depth of blue. Still, few would have anticipated the shout of pleasure which burst from the throats of the thousands of spectators present when the army of gymnasts deployed, charged, and then broke into the full run without a false movement being seen or the least deflection of line.

Lugano seemed to touch the high-water mark in more ways than one. Lugano is Italian in the richness of its nature and in the spirit and temperament of its people, and there was at once manifest a fine rivalry when these fine-built southerners came in touch with the stalwart Teutons of the northern slopes of the Alps, with the *élan* and verve of the men of the French cantons. This heightened the zest of the festival, gave it a touch of emotion not often present, and it was thought that there would never be another Lugano. But when it was seen at Schaffhausen that the number of competitors had increased—being only one or two hundred short of four thousand—while the *exercises d'ensemble* were still as faultlessly executed, the entire mass of spectators broke into thunders of applause. And why? Because it was felt that men who could act together with such perfection of unanimity and discipline constituted a material of the rarest kind for national defence. And that is a thought ever uppermost in the mind of the patriot Swiss.

It is curious to note how the peculiar idiosyncrasy, or the native genius, of the various cantons makes itself felt from time to time, and as the need arises. To Aargau is due the honour of having suggested and started the Federal rifle-meeting; to Berne chiefly belongs the credit of keeping alive the national sport of wrestling; the Gruyères country is famous for its *Ranz des vaches*, Appenzell for its melodious *Jodel*, as, indeed, for its love of song generally. Hence it was fitting and in accordance with the genius of its people that Appenzell should take the lead in regard to the establishment of festivals of popular song.

The first event of the kind took place so long ago as 1825 at Speicher-Vögelinseck, not far from the Lake of Constance. It aroused the greatest enthusiasm, and other cantons were soon following the example of Appenzell. Then, while the Federal idea was, as it were, thick in air, a Federal *fête* of popular song—a kind of Swiss *Eisteddfod*—was inaugurated, and has continued ever since, holding its gatherings every two years, now in one town, now in another, and doing much not only to refine and elevate the people, but to encourage oneness of national sentiment and feeling. It is not many years since the President of the Confederation, at one of these meetings, praised these societies of popular song for having promoted unity where formerly division prevailed—that is, between town and village—and for having tended so largely to ennoble the Swiss people by disseminating a love of music.

They have certainly developed a passionate love of music among all classes, and have besides had the effect of bringing out not only a large number of excellent composers, but of producing also a multitude of very beautiful songs—songs which would no doubt have met with the warm approval of Luther, who, holding that "notes give life to words," thought "the composer ought not to set to music sentiments that are not worth the trouble of calling to life." How many are the songs that have proved, by the way they take hold of the hearts of the people, that they well deserve to be vivified by music may be witnessed, not only at the great festivals of song, but almost daily at the more local gatherings and *fêtes,* and in the homes of the people.

Such songs as *Stehe fest, O Vaterland!* ("Stand firm, O Fatherland"), *Siegesfeier der Freiheit* ("The Triumph of Liberty"), *Die Schlacht bei St. Jakob* ("The Battle of St. Jacob"—the Thermopylæ of Swiss history), the *Serment du Grütli, Auf der Kirchweih zu Schwyz* ("At the Church-feast of Schwyz"), *O mein Heimatland* ("O dear Home-land"), *Trittst im Morgenrot daher* ("Thither in the Rosy Morn thou goest"), etc., may be heard at well-nigh every musical gathering. The last especially has become a national hymn.

These songs are all of German-Swiss origin, and it must be confessed that German Switzerland bears the palm for this kind of talent, although *la Suisse romande* does not lag far behind. Nor is it in any way behind the other parts of the Fatherland in its love of music. This may be seen by any passing visitor who spends an evening in the English Garden at Geneva, or—a treat which foreigners more rarely enjoy—attends one of the frequent concerts of sacred music in the cathedral church of St. Peter. For this love of music is not confined to popular songs, but extends to, and has a deep root in, sacred compositions. This taste has been cultivated by generations of talented composers, and by the presence and encouragement of such men as Wagner, Liszt, and others of the foremost rank in the world of music. As in other countries, so in Switzerland, church music had, by the free introduction of melody, and by the use of instrumental accompaniment, become brilliant at the expense of what may be termed solidity. In other words, its note was superficiality rather than sincerity and depth, and while it pleased the many, those of simpler lives and truer instincts began to show signs of revolt. It was complained that what was called stylish music—*la chant stylé*—had almost put an end to the once popular music of the home and the familiar social gathering, to the no small regret of the more unsophisticated children of the mountain vales.

A striking instance of the reaction against this tendency was witnessed at a recent festival at Berne, when the mixed chorus of a *Gesangverein* (Vocal Union), the girls of which appeared in their quaint native costumes, took the audience by storm; the air's *Vreneli ab' em Guggisberg* in especial producing something like the effect of a sudden revelation. Such awakenings are always a healthy sign, and though there can be no going back wholly to the music of the past, it is ever well for the outworn giant of civilisation, like Antæus, to seek refreshment and a renewal at the breast of the great mother. Such a revival is, in particular, making itself felt in regard to church music: the societies of St. Cecilia all over the Confederation working with zeal for a return to the Gregorian chant and to the diatonic of the ancient music of the Church.

This, however, as a note by the way. As regards the Federal musical festivals, it is thought that they have in the past favoured too exclusively the cultivation of the male voice, to the detriment of mixed choirs, and it is probable that a change will be called for in this respect. There are those, indeed, who think that the Federal *fête* idea has been overdone, especially as regards these vocal societies, and that some reform or modification is necessary. At the last gathering, held at Berne in 1899, a huge building had to be erected to accommodate six thousand singers and ten thousand spectators. The effect produced by these great masses of voice was, of course, prodigious, but it was felt by many that this form of national rivalry is carried too far, and—considering that there are other Federal gatherings all tending to grow larger and larger—perhaps the criticism is justified.

There is still another kind of celebration very popular among these free and vigorous people, and that is the *Festspiel*. The *Festspiel* is the national drama of the Swiss; it takes place in the open air; and its whole aim and object is to glorify and keep in remembrance the great historical events of the country, and to rejoice the common heart by the representation of stirring scenes from the everyday life of the people. In the Middle Ages the Swiss, like other European people, had their carnivals (relics of a still more ancient time), their Mystery and Morality plays, and, as a growth from these, their "days of commemoration"; these latter being marked by public representations of events calculated to warm the patriotic heart. At Lumbrein, in the Romansch part of the Grisons, there is still a representation of our Lord's Passion, which is held every thirty years, the last performance whereof took place in 1882, when a very deep impression was made upon the large throng of spectators who witnessed it. There is still a survival of the old carnival plays to be seen in the canton of Berne, in what is known as the Shrove Monday procession (*Hirsmontagsumzug*). Formerly it comprised biblical dramas; later these—probably under Protestant influence—gave place to patriotic representations, and in particular to scenes from the life of William Tell. These were intermingled with the buffooneries of Merry-andrews and Jack-puddings, and with wild and often burlesque dances. As another type of the same sort of thing may be mentioned the *Fête des Vignerons* of Vevey, referred to in another place.

With the re-establishment of the Confederation on its old basis in the early part of last century, and the entrance into it of several new cantons, the *Festspiel* leapt into renewed life. In 1828, at Küssnacht, for instance, scenes from the life of Tell were represented beneath the open sky. More recently the people of Altstätten commemorated the battle of Stoss on the very scene of the fight. Gradually the taste for this more modern form of the *Festspiel* has extended, and with it has grown a desire to make its representations conform more rigidly to the laws of dramatic art. William Tell is a stock subject, Schiller's play being the text generally chosen. Cham, Brugg, and Altstätten, among other places, have distinguished themselves by staging it, so to speak, on its "native heath"; while at Altdorf and Hochdorf special buildings have been put up to accommodate these popular representations.

With the provision of such assessories, however, the special feature of the *Festspiel* disappears. It is essentially an outdoor performance, a thing for the winds to play on, and for the sunshine to illumine. When it ceases to be that it becomes the theatre simply, which is another matter.

The *Festspiel,* as at present understood, may be said to date from the year 1886, when a grand popular festival took place at Sempach in honour of the five hundredth anniversary of the battle in which Arnold of Winkelried performed the deed of valour celebrated in Wordsworth's lines:

> *He of battle-martyrs chief!*
> *Who, to recall his daunted peers,*
> *For victory shaped an open space,*
> *By gathering with a wide embrace,*

*Into his single heart, a sheaf
Of fatal Austrian spears.*

The old-time *Festspiel* consisted of a procession and a cantata; but in this instance the composer of the music for the occasion, Arnold, produced a full-blown drama, which was so ably and so artistically interpreted by the Lucerners that henceforth the *Festspiel* was a new thing. What was done at Sempach was improved upon at Schwyz in 1891 (August 1st and 2nd) on the occasion of the *fête* celebrating the birth of the Confederation, and at the festival commemorating the foundation of the city of Berne on the 23rd and 24th of the same month. In each case men of the highest talent prepared the music and words of the compositions, and in each case the dramatic ensemble was so vivid and lifelike, the scenes from which the nation took its birth, so to speak, so naturally and yet so powerfully depicted, that the spectators were stirred with the deepest emotion on seeing them.

Other similar celebrations followed in quick succession. Amongst them may be mentioned the *Festspiel* of Little Basel in 1893, in which Wackernagel and Franz Huber collaborated in the production of the words and music respectively. In 1895, on the occasion of the Federal *Tir* at Winterthur, a *Festspiel* was performed glorifying the history of that town, the text of the work being by Leonhardt Steiner, and the music by Lothar Kempter. In 1898, Neuchâtel celebrated the fifth centenary of the republic of Neuchâtel in twelve tableaux, the poem and the music respectively being the work of Philippe Godet and M. Lauber. The *Marche des Armourins* of this piece was justly admired, and has ever since been a popular favourite. *La Suisse romande* throws itself into these *Festspiele* with as much fervour and enthusiasm as the German-speaking cantons, and one of the most noted makers of them is A. Ribaux. His dramatic composition, *Julia Alpinula*, was played in the old Roman amphitheature at Avenches; his *Charles le Téméraire* at Grandson, the scene of the battle; and his third *Festspiel, Reine Berthe*, at Payerne, the scene of the legend which forms the theme of the piece. This latter was performed in 1899, and was greatly admired both for its fine declamatory passages and for its ballets and dances.

The same year a series of *Festspiele* took place in commemoration of the battles of the Swabian War. The first was held at Calven, and it speaks much for the entrancing nature of the performance that the spectators were enabled to sit it out in spite of a continuous downpour of rain.

The secret of the spell lay in the cunning use the authors had made of the songs, costumes, legends, and even of the games of the district celebrated. This *fête* was followed by one at Schwaderlock, in Thurgau, when the standards of all the cantons that had contingents at the battle of Dornach (1499) were seen upon the open-air stage near the ancient castle from which the fight took its name, mingling in the stirring scenes of turmoil and war which came up for representation. Then another phase of the same theme was celebrated by the people of Soleure on a meadow near their chief town. For the text of this *Festspiel* Adrian von Arx was responsible, as was A. Munzinger for that of Schwaderlock, and both plays were remarkable for that warlike movement and "go," which, mingled with song and the sharp staccato of the drum, never fail to fire the martial heart of the Swiss. The battle of Dornach was again celebrated in July of the present year, on the occasion of the festivities in commemoration of the entrance of Basel into the Confederation.

Other *fêtes* of the kind might be referred to, as, for instance, that of the Escalade, which the Genevese celebrate processionally every year on the night of December 11th and 12th; but enough has, perhaps, been said to show how largely the *Festspiel* figures in the life and habits of the Swiss, and how deep is the impression it is calculated to make upon the character of a people who, whatever their present faults and short-comings, can always point to a sturdy and heroic past, while today they still manifest strivings towards an ideal which greater nations might emulate to their advantage.

# Traditions and Popular Festivals in Switzerland[1]

*by Erich Schwabe*

Two special requests that come up regularly from publishers of Swiss travel literature are for a documentary film on Swiss popular customs and for a handy booklet on the same subject. We recently complied with the first and with the film "Im Laufe des Jahres," an unaffected, realistic inventory; we are meeting the second with the publication of this concise booklet, compiled by Dr. Erich Schwabe and designed by René Creux. The Swiss National Tourist Office takes all the more pleasure in presenting this edition because it was not prompted by organizations interested in prefabricated travel and stereotyped tourism; the demand for a list of old popular traditions came from the annually increasing circle of visitors who regard travel to another country as a mentally enriching experience that needs preparation; in other words, from those particularly appreciated guests who do not preach travel culture and practise mass tourism.

It is satisfying to note that, comparing the list published 15 years ago, and now out of print, with his 1971 publication, since that time not a single custom has had to be dropped from the list or written off as having lost some of its genuine character. Certainly, you can find in Switzerland, as in all countries specializing in travel in tourism, folklore-type shows which in all kinds of establishments present the lightning tourist with a pseudo-folklore Switzerland dressed in its Sunday suit, or maybe having its Sunday nap. The superficial traveller will not get below the surface.

This booklet has nothing in common with such shows. It contains hardly a single custom introduced, distorted, or "updated" for the sake of tourism. Homstrom, Gidio Hosenstoss, Greth-Schell, the bénichons, Meitlisunntig, the Geneva Feuillus, the Roitschäggättä, and the

---

[1] Reprinted by permission of Switzerland Tourism, 1971.

Maggiolatas—none of these depends on a tourist background. In fact the Basel people would much rather keep their Fasnacht entirely to themselves and stage it without "foreigners"—meaning primarily their fellow-Swiss from Zurich. In recent years several customs which had dropped into oblivion have actually been revived—and this in Swiss cities—like the Räbeliechtli procession or the Wollishof Kläuse in Zürich. No doubt this is because even when living in a big city the Swiss thinks in terms of small districts and so in keeping up the old traditions he hopes to stimulate not tourism but local pride.

This booklet does not claim to be, and cannot be, more than a selection from the rich range of Swiss traditions and popular customs to which the Swiss Folklore Society, in particular, devotes regular and detailed publications. Festivals and traditions follow the course of the year in Switzerland's 3,000 communes, the smallest with 11 inhabitants and the biggest with 450,000. To complete the picture, a few church festivals have also been included, although these represent, as a letter correctly informs us, not merely traditions but the solemn profession of a faith with deep popular roots.

Christoph Bernoulli says that Appenzell peasant art is so very Appenzell that it is hardly Swiss any more—an indication of how, in looking at the richness of popular tradition, little Switzerland can be scaled down even further and its multiplicity multiplied. The Swiss people, given rather to solemnity and good old-fashioned application to the job in hand, have thought up so many festive occasions to offset their precise and reliable daily work, that sometimes it is said in jest that if someone covered Switzerland with canvas at the weekend, it would be one enormous fête marquee. This Switzerland *en fête* is the natural counterbalance to Switzerland at work. It almost seems that Goethe was thinking of the Swiss and their simultaneous pleasure in work and in festivals when he wrote:

*The daily round! evenings jest!*
*Week of labour! joyful zest!*

Dr. Werner Kämpfen
Director, Swiss National Tourist Office

## 1. THE TURN OF THE YEAR

In Switzerland as in many other countries, the New Year is ushered in with a unique blend of quiet reflection on the past and the future, with solemn ceremony and boisterous gaiety.

Switzerland is also one of the countries in which official New Year receptions are traditional. In Berne, the federal capital, the Diplomatic Corps ceremonially calls on the Federal President to pay its respects, a custom which is now not held on New Year's Day itself but a few days afterwards. In addition, the turn of the year in Switzerland is characterised by a colourful variety of popular traditions varying from region to region and each reflecting the character of the local people.

The fact that the year both ends and begins in the depths of winter is not fortuitous. Early on, in the time of their Republic, the Romans moved the New Year from March 1 to the closing days of the Saturnalia, one of their most important feasts.

The Teutons, too, felt the need for noise at this time of the year, when the days are shortest and the nights longest; they were protecting themselves against the lurking powers of evil and the avenging spirits of the dead during this dark and gloomy period.

## 2. THE "KLÄUSE" OF APPENZELL

The noisy antics of large or small groups, prancing figures clanging bells and sometimes wearing masks, are a relic of pagan beliefs not completely eradicated by the Festival of Christmas. This activity reaches its climax on New Year's Eve, although it starts long before Christmas and does not subside until the middle of January.

The "Silvesterkläuse" of Canton Appenzell-Ausserrhoden are among the most striking of these figures. Their name is an illusion to

St. Nicholas. Here, as in several other districts of Eastern Switzerland, his status of sainthood was apparently taken away by the Reformation and his appearance postponed until the end of the year.

The "Silvesterkläuse" are especially active in the Commune of Urnäsch: these masked, noisy groups, wearing magnificent headdresses, frolic around demanding money from the onlookers. Their artistic headgear often resembles filigree work, or depicts entire houses or landscapes.

On January 13, corresponding to the Old New Year's Eve of the Julian Calendar, they give a repeat performance.

## 3. "Greiflet" in Schwyz

On the evening of Epiphany, the lads don white herdsmen's blouses and in noisy procession circle the fountains of Schwyz . . . an ancient fertility ceremony.

## 4. Engadine "Schlitteda"

In Canton Grisons well-known New Year traditions are linked, in origin at least, with an institution that once was undoubtedly of some importance throughout Switzerland: the so-called "Knabenschaften" or boys' associations.

According to the Grisons historian G. Caduff, these are strictly private, rigidly organised guilds to which all unmarried men in a village belong from the time they leave school until they are wed.

In nearly all cases the social activities of the "Knabenschaften" are nowadays well to the fore. They organise popular festivals and are the main upholders of many customs and traditions.

The influence of the one-time guilds can be seen behind the Engadine "Schlittedas," in which every winter, on fine Sundays, the unmarried girls and boys pair up and, dressed in local costume, go on gay horse-drawn sleigh trips from village to village, to the accompaniment of music.

It was always the job of these organisations to encourage friendly relations between the sexes—but also to keep an eye on these relations; in fact they claimed the sole right to do this.

## 5. The Three Kings and Their Star

On Epiphany, January 6, Christian customs mingle with usages which are wholly archaic and reminiscent of pagan practices.

The noisy, money-soliciting parades contrast with the procession of the three kings with their star, illuminated from the inside. The custom has a special charm when it is kept up by smaller, or even very tiny groups, the intimate character of the event being to a certain extent preserved.

The celebrations are held in connection with Epiphany (evening of January 5 or 6). The custom is widespread in the Lucerne Plateau—Beromünster or the villages of Grosswangen, Nebikon and Schöts . . . in the Aargau Freiamt (such as in Boswil), in South Ticino, in the Rhine Valley district of St. Gall and especially in Canton Grisons, from the Vorderrhein and Hinterrhein Valleys (Bonaduz, Domat/Ems, region of Ilanz, Obervaz, Mulegns and Tinizong in the Oberhalbstein) over to the Misox and the Calanca.

In Canton Valais, the custom is nowadays carried on only in the Lötschental, where the white-clad kings with a small escort, including the starbearer, "gallop" through the villages on beautifully-carved hobby horses.

## 6. Women and Girls Celebrate in the Seetal

On "Meitlisunntig," the second Sunday in January, the girls of Meisterschwanden and Fahrwangen, in the Seetal district of Aargau, state a procession in historical uniforms and a military parade before a . . . feminine . . . "General Staff." This is followed by a popular festival.

According to tradition, the custom goes back to the Villmergen War of 1712. The women of both communes are said to have given vital help that led to the victory of the Protestant Bernese over the Catholic forces of Central Switzerland.

## 7. "VOGEL GRYFF" IN BASEL

The annual festival of the three guilds—known as "Companies of Honour"—of Kleinbasel, the part of Basel city on the right bank of the River Rhine, falls on the 13th, the 20th, or the 27th of January, depending on which Company is presiding.

The three emblematic figures of the companies, Griffin, Wild Man and Lion, meet up after the Wild Man has travelled down the Rhine on a raft.

Their reunion takes place at midday and they dance and caper on the Central Rhine Bridge to the beat of drums. In the afternoon they give several repeat performances as they parade through the streets.

## 8. ST. SEBASTIAN AT FINHAUT (VALAIS)

Marking the Patronal Festival on January 20, two huge and richly decorated cakes are borne in solemn procession to the church and later divided up among members of the congregation.

## 9. "HOMSTROM" AT SCUOL

The ceremony that takes place on the first Sunday in February at Scuol in the Lower Engadine can be regarded as a kind of forerunner to the bonfires lit throughout many parts of Switzerland at Carnival time.

On several poles up to 30 feet high, the youngsters plait big bales of straw into the shape of "straw men" (Homstrom). These are carried with enthusiasm to various easily-visible points above the upper and lower village, to be delivered up the flames in the evening as a symbol of winter's imminent departure.

## 10. CARNIVAL CUSTOMS GALORE

An unusually rich variety of carnival traditions are carried on from the middle of January to Ash Wednesday and beyond. In certain districts they are numerous. In others such as West Switzerland or the Berne Region, they are less important or were wholly suppressed by the Reformation.

Yet it is a Protestant city, that stages the biggest and best-known carnival event in the whole of Switzerland. In East and Central Switzerland especially, the tradition has been upheld practically without interruption.

The reason for this variation throughout the country is found not least in the origins, differing from region to region, of the individual carnival customs, characterised by no less than five main features.

The one dating farthest back to ancient times is the masked frolics, parades, and capers. Apparently nourished by ancient primitive beliefs, this aspect is again reinforced towards the end of winter. Along with this has become linked the customs of poking cheerful fun originally probably directed at the vagaries of the outgoing "bad" season, and later extended to cover all kinds of human weaknesses and stupidities.

## 11. LÖTSCHENTAL "ROITSCHÄGGÄTTÄ"

Wearing fierce wooden masks and clad in goat and sheep skins, the "Roitschäggättä" roister through the villages of the Lötschental on "Dirty Thursday," noisy and fearsome figures.

## 12. CARNIVAL IN CANTON SCHWYZ

In Canton Schwyz, characteristic figures appear on Carnival Monday or Tuesday: in the town of Schwyz, the "Nüssler," in Einsiedeln the bread-throwing "Joheen," etc.

## 13. Lucerne's "Fritschi" Parade

Participation of the ancient guilds is an additional element in the city of Lucerne's carnival customs. On "Dirty Thursday" the Master of the "Safran" Guild appears as the masked figure of "Father Fritschi" and in this role distributes gifts to welfare organisations.

In the afternoon the entire "Fritschi" family makes its appearance on a wagon to take part in the big humorous parade. This is repeated—featuring another Guild—on Carnival Monday, but without "Fritschi."

## 14. Risotto Meal in the Ticino

An important pointer to the origin of Carnivaltide customs lies in the efforts of the medieval Church—unable to abolish the mask usages rooted in pagan times—to counter them by fixing them to take place before the time of strict fasting. This meant that the people could again eat heartily and celebrate before the fast days.

This is the background to the free risotto meal, once a social institution, which is served to the local people in the Ticino's bigger localities at Carnival time.

## 15. "Greth-Schell" in Zug

In Zug, too, a guild carries on a Carnival Monday custom: that of "Greth-Schell," a masked feminine figure carrying her husband in a basket on her back.

## 16. Carnival Bonfires

Throughout many regions of Switzerland, usually on "Old Carnival," the Sunday after Ash Wednesday, the carnival bonfires are lit at night. In German-speaking places they are called "Fasnachtsfunken" and in West Switzerland are known as "brandons."

In Carnival tradition the bonfires represent portents of Spring and are symbolic of Winter's downfall. In many places in Canton Zurich,

Winter is personified in the form of a straw figure—the "Böögg"—which is burned. The "Böögg" figures in the "Sechseläuten" celebrations in the city of Zurich later in the year.

## 17. CARNIVAL TIME IN THE ST. GALL RHINE VALLEY AND SEZTAL

In the carnival events, especially those in the Sargans district, the "Knabenschaften" mentioned earlier in connection with the "Schlitteda" custom are still responsible for certain organisational tasks. Typical masks can be seen at Flums, Berschis, and Walenstadt.

By contrast, at Altstätten in the Rhine Valley, the "Röllelibützen" in their neat costumes give an impression of almost courtly elegance. During their processions on Carnival Monday and Tuesday they carry water sprays with which they give bystanders a good sprinkling.

## 18. "GIDIO HOSENSTOSS" AT HERISAU (APPENZELL-AUSSERRHODEN)

The bogeyman to be burned is sometimes accused of a long list of sins. This is what happens at Herisau when "Gidio Hosenstoss" is given a satirical funeral on Ash Wednesday.

## 19. HURLING THE DISC

An especially pleasant tradition, nourished on the Carnival bonfire, has been kept up in a few places in East and North-West Switzerland.

It takes place on the Sunday before Ash Wednesday at Matt in the Sernf Valley of Glarus, and on the Sunday after at Wartau in St. Gall, Untervaz, and Danis-Tavanasa in the Rhine Valley of Graubünden, at Benken and Biel (Canton Basel-Country) and in several communes of the Jura district of Northern Solothurn. "Disc hurling" is a privilege reserved for schoolboys. At night, to the accompaniment of a dedication they hurl red-hot wooden discs over a mountainside, far into the valley.

## 20. "LICHTERSCHWEMMEN"

The "Lichterschwemmen" is a custom still to some extent closely linked with the fire tradition but not usually observed until the third Sunday before Easter at Unterengstringen near Zurich, at Ellikon (Zurich), Islikon in Thurgau, and Ermensee in the Seetal District of Lucerne.

Little wooden rafts bearing candles are put out in the evening to float on the village stream or, at Unterengstringen, on the River Limmat. The ceremony is accompanied by songs from the youngsters of the village, music from the local band, and, occasionally, by a modest firework display.

## 21. "AESCHLIBUEBE" AT ELGG (ZURICH)

The "Aeschlibuebe" custom is observed on Ash Wednesday, with a morning and afternoon march by cadets. The custom originates from the days when the men liable for military service paraded for an arms inspection.

## 22. BASEL FASNACHT

Basel's biggest and best-loved popular festival, the "Fasnacht" gets off to an impressive start at four o'clock in the morning with the "Morgenstreich," and includes processions of the bigger and smaller "cliques," each one wittily lampooning a certain subject or event, the evening "Schnitzelbank" presentations in the restaurants, and other amusements.

The "Fasnacht" goes on from the Monday after Ash Wednesday

until the small hours of Thursday, ebbing and flowing in intensity and several times interrupting the normal routine of daily work.

Monday between four and six o'clock, Monday and Wednesday afternoon, and the evenings are the high points of activities whose complexity suggests that the custom has developed from a number of different sources.

The core of the more recent development, in the nineteenth century, was formed by the associations of the old city and the suburbs, precursors of the present-day "cliques," and above all by the drums and fifes, a legacy of foreign mercenary service, which have been perfected to their present remarkable precision.

An art in itself is the painting of the huge transparent lanterns.

## 23. GROPPENFASNACHT AT ERMATINGEN (THURGAU)

On the third Sunday before Easter, Ermatingen, on the Untersee in North-East Switzerland, celebrates the "Groppenfasnacht," often with a big parade in which the central feature is a "Gropp" (a well-known fish).

## 24. CHALANDA MARZ

The "Chalanda Marz" custom is widely observed on March 1 in the Lower and Upper Engadine, the Oberhalbstein and still further north on the Lenzerheide. It is a springtime tradition, in which the young people, some dressed in fancy costumes, greet the coming of the season with the ringing of bells, ranging from tiny editions to the outsize varieties, and with the cracking of whips.

The demons of winter could hardly be symbolically driven away at a better time than this, a time when the warmth of Spring is already beginning to pervade the sunny high valleys.

The custom is linked with a rite obviously held in high importance back in ancient times, as is also indicated by the date, which was an important one in the Roman calendar. The tradition can be observed at its most unspoiled and best in the Upper Engadine. In the morning, and sometimes again in the afternoon, there is a procession with well-defined features. It includes a garlanded sleigh pulled by six lads acting as "horses," the costumed leaders of the party, and the bell-swinging schoolboys who bring up the rear. In front of each house there is singing, and gifts are collected.

## 25. Neuchâtel Commemorates its Constitution

On March 1, Canton Neuchâtel commemorates the storming of the capital and the proclamation of the Republic (1848) with artillery salutes, parades, and patriotic demonstrations.

## 26. Palm Sunday Observances

In Roman Catholic areas of East and Central Switzerland, richly decorated "palms" (mostly holly or other branches) are blessed in church; according to tradition they protect farm and pastures.

## 27. The Mendrisio Good Friday Processions

Processions are among the most ardent and sincere aspects of life among the people of the Ticino.

Yet the southern character of the Ticinesi means that even the most solemn Passion scenes, as presented in such places as Locarno, Bignasco, Ronco, or Mendrisio, not only fill spectators with reverence for the meaning of what is being enacted, but also with innocent pleasure at the beauty and colour of the procession itself.

The two well-known Mendrisio processions, on the evenings of Maundy Thursday and Good Friday, are basically different in character. The first may be regarded as an example of the most primitive dramatic art. Christ's journey to Calvary is re-enacted in exaggerated fashion and the procession, with its baroque undertones, includes the various characters of the Passion story, some of them in glittering attire and trappings, others in modest, simple dress.

The second procession, however, is strongly liturgical. The moving play-acting of the previous evening gives way to a dignified procession of the clergy. Luminous banners which hang across the streets or are carried along in the procession give it additional character.

## 28. Egg Races

A number of spring symbols represent the new life sprouting in the warmth and sun. One of the most important of these is the egg, which is the central feature of Easter fun and games.

In North-West Switzerland, in rural Basel and on the Bözberg, as well as in the Bernese lakeland district, egg racing is a well-established custom on Easter Monday and, more often, again on the Sunday after Easter.

This is a contest in which one competitor has to carry a large number of eggs a certain distance before the other one has completed a run to the next village.

## 29. Easter Alms

At Ferden in the Lötschental, goatsmilk cheese, bread and wine are distributed to parishioners on Easter Monday, soon after midday. The distribution is a bequest going back to the Middle Ages and was originally endowed to avert harm from three alps whose milk yield on July 23 and 24 is still reserved for the purpose.

Similar benefactions, based on other provisions, can also be found elsewhere in Canton Valais: at Hérémence and Savièse at Easter, at Sembrancher at Whitsun and at Kippel on the Feast of All Souls.

## 30. The Näfels Prilgrimage

The Näfels Pilgrimage, the annual commemoration of the Battle of Näfels, fought on April 9, 1388, is one of the main festivals of Canton Glarus and takes place on the first Thursday in April.

Two groups start off from Glarus early in the morning; one is a Catholic procession, with church banners, crucifixes, clergy and Capuchin monks, and the other includes the united male voice choirs and band and Protestant citizens—the Protestants being in the majority in Glarus. Both groups make a pilgrimage to the battlefield, near Scheisingen, where the *Landamman* or the *Landesstatthaldter* delivers the address.

Proceeding further towards Näfels, the Catholic procession halts briefly for prayers at each of the eleven memorial stones. At about 10 a.m. on the "Pilgrimage Square" at Näfels, the Cantonal Clerk reads out the "Pilgrimage Document" which contains the names of those killed in the battle. The festival sermon is preached on alternate years by Protestant and Catholic clergy.

In conclusion, there is a ceremony at the battle memorial and a solemn High Mass in Näfels Parish Church.

## 31. Zurich's "Sechseläuten"

This is the day of Zurich's big Spring festival. Originally the ceremony was held on the Monday following the Spring equinox, and was not transferred to a Monday in April until 1880.

The "Sechseläuten" stems from two different elements, the ancient Guild traditions connected with the inspection of the citizen militia, and the carnival bonfire with the ceremonial burning of the "Böögg," the symbol of winter.

The two elements were fused in the nineteenth century into the festival as it is known today. The ancient craft guilds and the much more recent suburban guilds are responsible for the organisation. This is a many-sided job, ranging from the hoisting of flags on the tower of St. Peter's to indicate that the children's procession will be held on Sunday afternoon, to the "pièce de résistance," which is the big, inventive, fancy dress parade on Monday afternoon, with the subsequent "execution" of the "Böögg," which is burned on the Sechseläutenplatz at six o'clock in the evening as the church bells chime, hence the name of the festival.

In the evening, there is more fun as the guildsmen march through the streets of the Old Town and call at each other's guildhouses.

## 32. LANDSGEMEINDEN

In five Swiss rural and mountain cantons, a tradition of a very special sort is observed at the end of April or the beginning of May. It is the *Landsgemeinde*, a deep-rooted example of democracy in its most genuine and vivid form.

The voters assembled in the "ring" elect their representative to the cantonal authorities and dispose of important business.

In four half-cantons, Appenzell Innerrhoden, Appenzell Ausserrhoden, Nidwalden and Obwalden, the *Landsgemeinden* meet on the last Sunday in April while in Glarus, the ceremony is held on the first Sunday in May. It is difficult to say which of these open-air meetings is the most impressive. The one in Appenzell Ausserrhoden—held at Hundwil in years with uneven end digits and at Trogen in the others—may appear particularly compact. On the other hand, the *Landsgemeinden* in Glarus (held in Glarus town), Obwalden (on the Landenberg near Sarnen), Nidwalden (at Wyl an der Aa, Stans), and Appenzell Innerrhoden (at Appenzell) are often marked by their free give-and-take of discussion and argument.

Every two years *Landsgemeinden*—some of them impressive affairs—are also held in certain districts of Canton Graubünden, although their functions appear to be restricted.

## 33. SINGING-IN MAY AT ZURICH

At a midnight ceremony on the Lindenhof in the heart of the city, Zurich students sing songs to welcome May.

## 34. "MAI-BÄREN" AT BAD RAGAZ

On the afternoon of the first Sunday in May, curious objects— carefully constructed wooden frames richly adorned with foliage and paper streamers—make their appearance in several quarters of Bad Ragaz.

Known as "Mai-Bären," they are carried around and finally some of them are thrown into the rushing waters of the Tamina.

The "Mai-Bären" symbolise crop demons and the custom reflects an ancient fertility rite. The youngsters who go around with them make a din with bells and collect donations for their school outing fund.

## 35. "Feuillu" in Canton Geneva

The charming children's custom of "Feuillu" is kept up on the first Sunday of May in several country districts of Geneva. The tradition centres on the "Bête," a framework covered with foliage, and is similar to the "Maibär" custom at Bad-Ragaz.

## 36. Ticino "Maggiolata"

On the first Sunday of May in many places in Ticino—especially the Lugano district—the children gather round a maypole and sing, a custom known as "Maggiolata."

## 37. The Vaudois "Abbayes"

Mostly held in May, the "Abbayes" of Canton Vaud are local festivals organised by the marksmen's clubs and centred around a shooting contest.

Very many of these events, especially in the urban areas, originated in the sixteenth century, and some go even further back. The shooting contest generally takes place on a Saturday but the accompanying local fête and parades, such as that of the "Abbaye des écharpes blanches" in Montreux, last over the whole weekend.

## 38. Stoss Pilgrimage in Appenzell

Not least among the many patriotic traditions kept up in Switzerland are those commemorating the victories won by the Confederates of old.

Every year around May 14, the people of Appenzell remember the battle for freedom on the Stoss, fought by their forefathers in 1405 against the Abbot of St. Gall and his allies.

Early in the morning, they proceed in a long procession from Appenzell to the Memorial Chapel on the pass leading into the Rhine Valley. Historical events are recalled and the ceremonies are followed by a shooting match.

## 39. Ladies' Shooting Contest at Entlebuch

Every third year, generally in the second half of May, Entlebuch, Escholzmatt and Schüpfheim, all in Canton Lucerne, take it in turn to stage the "Entlebuch Official and Ladies' Shooting Contest."

This is an important event lasting three days, in which the ladies have the right to take part, and do so in large numbers.

The official closing festival day falls on a Wednesday and includes a church service, a parade, the handing over of the official banner, and the distribution of prizes.

## 40. Ascension Day Ride

In pagan times when the Alemannic clan system held sway, ceremonies were held in the Spring in the fields to exorcise evil spirits and protect the growing crops.

The Christian Church instituted in place of these usages the ceremony of blessing the fields and crops, on the days before and on Ascension Day. From this developed the custom of pacing out the boundaries and sometimes riding round the parish bounds, a custom still maintained at *Beromünster*, Sempach, Hitzkirch, and a few other places, all in the Lucerne region.

The most colourful and best known of the Ascension Day rides, in which mounted clergy take part, is that of *Beromünster*, where the Chapter Canons, in their brightly coloured cloaks, take a leading part. From daybreak on, more than a hundred horsemen are out. The return to the beflagged little town is a particularly stirring sight, with all eyes on the impressive spectacle of the cavalcade.

Along the entire route, and in particular at the end of the route, huge arches of triumph are erected. Under these the clergy bestow their blessings, to the accompaniment of choir singing.

## 41. Pacing the Bounds in Rural Basel

As a result of the Reformation, what were originally religious processions round the boundaries, developed in Rural Basel into a purely secular inspection of the bounds. As a rule, these also take place before or on Ascension Day, and are generally the occasion for holding fêtes in the communes.

The most important of them is the "Banntag" at Liestal, held on the Monday before Ascension Day. The citizens set off at 8 o'clock in the morning, and march along the boundaries to the beat of drums, adding to the fun by firing off pistols and muskets.

## 42. Corpus Christi

The Feast of Corpus Christi, introduced by Pope Urban IV in 1264, is observed everywhere in the Roman Catholic regions of Switzerland with great pomp and ceremony on the second Thursday after Whitsun.

Nature, now in full bloom, provides much of the decoration that adorns the houses and the streets through which the impressive processions pass, starting from and returning to the main church of the locality. On the way, they halt at open-air altars for the Gospel to be read and for blessings to be bestowed as artillery salvoes boom out. Because of their size and the great variety of groups taking part, the processions in the towns and cities of important monastery villages are the most impressive—as at Einsiedeln or Lucerne, Fribourg or Sion, where they centre on the clergy, led by the Bishop, and on the secular authorities with the entire cantonal government. In the smaller places, by contrast, it is often the attractive festive regional costumes worn by the women that particularly catch the eye. The processions at Appenzell and Düdingen near Fribourg are worth special mention.

## 43. Benediction Sunday

In some parts of Canton Valais, "Benediction Sunday" is celebrated in addition to Corpus Christi. Various mountain villages observe this custom with arrangements which are as elaborate as those for Corpus Christi and sometimes even more so.

The very name "Benediction Sunday" indicates the central purpose of the festival—to ask a blessing on the crops now in full growth.

Especially well-known is the observance of this custom in the Lötschental region. On the Sunday after Corpus Christi, the parish of Kippel observes Benediction Sunday in the morning, and the parish of Blatten celebrates in the afternoon.

Starting from the church, the procession winds through the narrow, crooked lanes out into the countryside. In the centre of the procession, beneath a canopy, is the priest with the Host. The women of Lötschental add colour and charm to the procession with their decorative local costumes, but the main eye-catchers are undoubtedly the "Lord's Grenadiers," who march along in uniforms of Napoleon's time, and escort the big church banners.

## 44. JUNE THE FIRST IN GENEVA

On June 1 each year the City of Geneva commemorates the landing of troops from Fribourg and Solothurn at Port Noir in 1814, an event which was to bring Geneva and its people freedom as part of the Swiss Confederation after the confusion of the Napoleonic period. A colourful procession which includes the authorities, local organisations, and bands makes its way to Port Noir for simple ceremonies.

## 45. ASCENT TO SUMMER PASTURES

The structure of mountain agriculture and the important share of it contributed by cattle and dairy farming, are also reflected in the customs of the mountain folk.

The mountain dweller's yearly round is largely determined by the need to make sure that he also fully uses the upper areas available for husbandry, namely, the higher meadows and above these the alpine pastures. High points of the year are the driving of the cattle up to the alpine pastures and the return down to the valleys in the autumn, with, possibly, visits paid to the alp in between by the owner or the alpine farming co-operative, as the case may be.

The ceremony of driving up the cattle, in particular, is extremely appealing, especially in regions where the herdsman's traditional way of life is still firmly rooted. Such places are the Gruyère or Appenzell regions, where the people still keep up a strong interest in local costumes, where implements and utensils are still carved from wood, and where the characteristic yodeling of the cowmen is still heard in its natural setting. In a long drawn-out column, the cattle pass through the villages of the valley, climbing up stagewise by way of steep tracks.

The procession is led by the decorated "queen" cow, with her huge bell. She is followed by the rest of the herd, by the herdsmen, and the carts carrying the utensils needed up on the alp, with the small livestock bringing up the rear.

### 46. Cow Fights in Valais

In Canton Valais, a special feature of the ascent to the alpine pastures are the cow fights. The small, black, short-horned Eringer breed raised in the Canton engage in real trials of strength.

Strong, wiry and agile, the cows thrust at each other and the one that succeeds in keeping all her rivals at bay is given the honour of being the leading or "queen" cow during the period on the Alp—and as such is treated with due respect.

### 47. Commemorating the Battle of Morat

The little walled town of Morat has played a decisive part in Swiss history. It was here that, on June 22, 1476, the Confederates were victorious over Charles the Bold of Burgundy, laying a basis for the French-speaking areas to become Swiss. June 22 is still especially meaningful for the youngsters of Morat, for the anniversary of the battle is commemorated as a children's festival, with church service, ceremonial parade, and general fun. The widespread tradition of children's festivals assumes special significance at Morat.

## 48. CHILDREN'S FESTIVALS

With the beginning of midsummer, a host of children's festivals are held throughout French-Switzerland and German-Switzerland. As their names reveal, some of them have developed from spring customs into meaningful, gay occasions immediately before the summer pause.

They are part of a well-entrenched tradition especially in places which have no other striking annual customs.

The four most important such festivals in Canton Aargau are the "Rutenzug" in Brugg on the second Thursday in July, the "Maienzug" in Aarau on the second Friday in July, and the youth festivals of Lenzburg and Zofingen, held partly on the same dates. These festivals combine a procession, including schoolgirls in snow-white dresses, a ceremony in the city church or in the open air on the festival ground, with exercises by cadets and lively dancing and games.

The "Solennität" at Burgdorf on the last Monday in June is similar. In West Switzerland—at Neuchâtel, Lausanne, or Geneva—there may be minor differences, but the idea, the spirit and the charm remain the same everywhere.

## 49. THE ST. GALL CHILDREN'S FESTIVAL

The children's festival in the East Swiss commercial centre of St. Gall is easily the most notable event of its kind in Switzerland. In its present form it goes back to 1824 and is generally held every two years at the end of June or the beginning of July.

In an impressive procession, which might at the same time be described as a festival parade of St. Gall's textile and embroidery products, up to ten thousand schoolchildren make their way to the Rosenberg for entertainments of all kinds.

## 50. Sempach Battle Commemoration

On the morning of the Monday after July 4, the Lucerne Government, military and student delegations, and historical groups make their way in solemn procession to the battlefield of 1386. The commemorative address is given by the memorial stone, opposite the battle chapel. After this, the battle report is read and a solemn service held in the chapel. After the return to Lucerne, the student organisations stage an evening procession.

## 51. Feast of St. Placidus in Disentis

On the feast day of the local patron saint, St. Placidus, there is a big procession in which some thirty reliquaries are carried from the Monastery to the parish church and back.

## 52. Dornach Battle Commemoration

The victory at Dornach in 1499 is remembered on the battlefield itself and in the city of Solothurn on the Sunday nearest to July 22. At Dornach there is a big commemorative festival every five years. In Solothurn, the St. Margrithen Brotherhood, based in the suburb on the right bank of the River Aare, keeps up the annual custom of the "Vorstädterkilbi." This includes a church service, a procession and act of commemoration as well as the high point of the day, the "Kilbi" dancing in the afternoon on the Aare bridges and in the suburban streets.

## 53. Alp Festivals

Cattle owners mostly choose the middle of summer to pay visits to the herdsmen up on the alp. In the Vaud Alps this custom is known as "mi-été," and the occasion has always been marked by jolly get-togethers which have turned into small festivals.

A long time ago there obviously developed from these the "Bergsdorfet" as they are called in the Bernese Oberland and "Suuffsunntig," the term used especially in the Saanen region. "Suuff" or "Schluck" is the term used for the viscous milk which has been curdled with rennet in the cheesemaking vat.

They consist of gay and lively mountain fêtes held on an open-air stage, with flag-swinging, alphorn blowing, and also an alpine-style wrestling match.

In fact the major alpine events on the Grosse Scheidegg and the Männlichen, on the Brünig Pass and on the Hahnenmoos, are famous for their wrestling festivals, held as they have been since olden times on the summits of the passes linking the valleys, or on the mountain ridges—friendly encounters and trials of strength. In the Saanen region every alp has its "Suuffsunntig" and its highlight is the parading of the "queen" cow, garlanded and adorned for the occasion. The dates of these events change, and are fixed from year to year.

## 54. Alpine Religious Services

Largely for the mountain dwellers, alpine services were once held in conjunction with the "Bergdorfet," and still are at the "Mi-été" festivals in the Vaud Alps (Taveyannaz, Jaman). In the Bernese Oberland the festivals and the services have long been held separately, generally early on Sunday mornings in July or August. Of special interest is the Gastern Service near Kandersteg, at 11 a.m. on the first Sunday in August. At this service the parson from Kandersteg reads the text out of the big Gastern Bible of 1696.

## 55. "Maria Zum Schnee"

In Catholic districts, Mass is celebrated on August 5 in the chapels dedicated to Our Lady of the Snows (Rigi-Klösterli, Meglisalp, Bettmeralp, Schwarzsee ob Zermatt).

## 56. "Bergsonntag" in the Grisons

Mountain fêtes are also held on the alpine meadows of northern Graubünden (Grisons) at midsummer. Known as "Bergsonntag," this festival includes a service, music, dancing, and wrestling.

## 57. August 1: Swiss National Day

Swiss National Day, commemorating the pact made by the three original cantons in 1291, is celebrated on August 1, when in town and country alike parades and patriotic gatherings are held, at some of which the wording of the historic pact is read out. Celebrations to mark the coming of age of young citizens are also often held on this day. In the evening fireworks criss-cross the sky. Bonfires are lit on the hills and mountains, superseding those which in some places used to mark the Feast of St. James, July 25.

National Day is a fairly recent tradition; it has only been observed since the 600th anniversary of the Swiss Confederation was celebrated in 1891.

## 58. Lüdern-Chilbi

Mountain fêtes are also held in the Emmental. The best-known is the "Lüdern-Chilbi," on Sunday, August 10, or the Sunday after that date. It is popular for its wrestling and dancing.

## 59. Horse Market and Racing at Saignelégier

The Franches-Montagnes comprise some of the finest countryside in the Jura region and are among the horse-breeding centres of Switzerland. Important horse markets are held here: the senior one, restricted purely to horse dealing, at Chaindon near Reconvilier, held on the first Monday in September, and the horse show, founded in 1897 at Saignelégier, usually held on the second weekend of August.

At the latter, dealing tends to take second place to the presentation and judging of the Franches-Montagnes stallions, mares, and foals, for which visitors come from all over Switzerland. The animals are divided into three quality classes: the finest horses appear late on Sunday morning in a parade which always earns admiration. On Sunday afternoon high points of the event are the festive parade, depicting local cattle and horse breeding, and above all, extremely popular horse racing events. Farmers' sons and daughters, racing on waggons drawn by one or more horses, or trying their luck riding their mounts bareback, take part in a thrilling contest. After this come trotting events and military races.

## 60. SHEPHERDS' FESTIVALS

Summer traditions also spring from sheep farming, although this has now greatly declined in Switzerland. Typical shepherds' festivals are still held in the highest alpine grazing zones, such as that on the Daubensee by the Gemmi Pass on the second Sunday in August, which retains its genuine character. There is also the "Schafscheid," a ceremony at which the sheep are returned to their owners after the summer grazing. This is often a very attractive occasion and among the places it can be seen is Riffenmatt near Guggisberg, on the first Thursday of September.

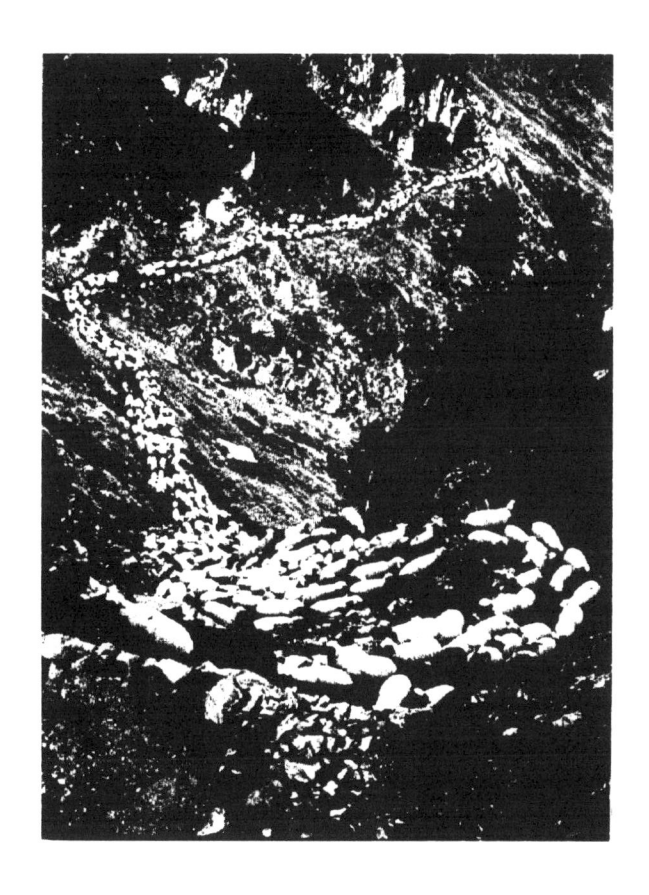

## 61. Blessings and Tithes on the Alps

In the Valais as in other areas, the priest walks the fields to invoke a Divine blessing on the crops and visits each and every alp blessing pastures, cowsheds, and animals. In return, the alpine farmers make a donation to the Church in the form of dairy produce. This custom, based perhaps upon the ancient tithe system, is kept up on the Sunday after the Feast of St. Bartholomew, August 24, at Vissoie, main locality of the Anniviers Valley, where the herdsmen bring the priest charmingly decorated cheeses in a prescribed sequence.

## 62. Cheese Distribution in the Justis Valley

In the Justis Valley, near Relingen and Sigriswil above the Lake of Thun, the custom known as "Käseteilet" is linked with the driving down of the cattle from the alpine pastures, which takes place towards the end of September. The precise date of the "Käseteilet" is fixed by the local presidents and stewards, the men who look after the economic side of things on the four alps of the valley. Farmers who possess mountain rights assemble with their families on the "Spycherbärg," with its four cheese storage huts, each belonging to one of the alps. The cheeses are there piled up in "lots." To each mountain right is assigned one "lot," that is, the yield of one cow throughout one summer. Generally this amounts of five cheeses, weighing from 20 to 30 pounds, with older, medium-aged and young cheeses being put together. First comes a speech by the steward and the announcement of the yield from each alp. Then, to avoid unfairness, a draw is held to apportion the share of each owner of mountain rights.

Then there is a small festival, and, in the early afternoon, the alpine folk make their way down to the valley. The cattle follow in the evening, and the cow with the best yield from each alp is specially spruced up and decorated.

## 63. "Kilbi" and "Bénichon"

After the harvest and the return of the cattle from the high pastures many places keep up the tradition of holding a "Kilbi" or fête. Originally held to mark the anniversary of the church consecration or the Feast of the church's patron saint, the "Kilbi" has in most localities lost its religious significance, and is marked by dancing and amusements of every kind. The equivalent in Canton Fribourg is the "Bénichon," held around Fribourg on the second Sunday in September, and in the Gruyère district on the second Sunday in October, while in Canton Ticino the festival is known as the "Sagra," and is more religious in character.

## 64. "Bachfischet" in Aarau

After the bed of the town brook has been cleaned, the stream is led back into its channel, generally at the beginning of September, and it is welcomed by an escort of youngsters with singing, music, and a lantern procession.

## 65. Zurich "Knabenschiessen"

Shooting events are among the most important of the autumn traditions, and the Zurich Boys' Shooting Contest held over the second weekend in September is one of the biggest. Its origins go back to medieval shooting matches held for lads who had practised the art of marksmanship during the summer.

At the Albisgütli butts, 53 targets are in continuous use on Saturday and Sunday afternoons and on Monday morning. The best boy marksman is honoured with the title of "King" of the contest.

## 66. "Ausschiesset" in Thun

The Thun "Ausschiesset" takes place after the beginning of the autumn holidays—end of September or beginning of October. This custom goes back to 1551 and its present-day form has changed little since the eighteenth century.

Parades, shooting contests, and the "Gessler Shoot" for crossbow marksmen are held from Sunday to Tuesday. Characteristic figure—representing the "Pritschenmeister" who in the old days used to see that order was kept—is the "Fulehung," which romps through the streets in a devil's mask.

## 67. "Stecklitragen" at Wil (St. Gall)

On the first or second Sunday of October, the young people of Wil (St. Gall) stage an appealing procession in which they carry, attached to poles, the gifts for the final shootings match of the field guards.

## 68. Grape Harvest Festivals

Grape harvest time in the wine-growing areas is a busy but cheerful time of the year for all concerned, and linked with the harvest in some centres are large-scale annual festivals, lively affairs held on the last Sunday in September or the first Sunday in October.

The festivals of Sierre in Canton Valais and Morges, on the Lake of Geneva, certainly rank high on the list, while in the Ticino, Lugano stages an event which gets more popular every year. As at Sierre and Morges, the central feature is a well-organised festive parade.

The grape-harvest festival at Neuchâtel is one of the popular major festivals held in different cities. The parade, here also the central feature of the tradition, was first held in 1902 and has been constantly improved year by year.

Nowadays the confetti battles and masks, and the amusements and dancing on Saturday and Sunday evenings are also big attractions. Market stalls and little booths serving drinks are put in the streets, and some of the city's fountains are even transformed into novel "wineshops."

## 69. "Lesesonntage" on the Lake of Bienne

In the wine-growing villages and little towns on the northern shore of the Lake of Bienne, five "Lesesonntage" are held on successive

Sundays, with all the fun of a festival and sometimes parades as well.

## 70. Alpine Popular Festivals

The "Älplerkilbi" or Alpine popular festivals of Central Switzerland take place in the second half of October or the first half of November and hold a particularly important place in local traditions in Obwalden and Nidwalden. At these festivals a solemn service of thanksgiving contrasts with the general light-hearted atmosphere, witty addresses given by the "two savages," and dancing galore.

The masked "savages" ("Wildma" and "Wildwyb") represent mountain spirits once supposed to have roamed the alpine meadows and crags.

## 71. "Räbenlichter"

Throughout Canton Zurich at the beginning of November it is the custom to hollow out newly-harvested turnips, carve designs on the outside and make lanterns out of them by lighting a candle inside. This custom has roots in ancient times; as the year approached its end, the light was supposed to help ward off the powers of darkness.

Originally the "Räbenliechtli" were generally carried around or displayed single. But over the years, especially in recent decades, the custom has been broadened and now includes evening processions—some big, some small—by schoolchildren in many districts, especially in the Zürcher Unterland (Bülach, Regensberg, Eglisau, etc.) and also in the suburbs of Winterthur and the city of Zurich (including Wollishofen, Wipkingen, and Wiedikon).

In Richterswil on the Sunday nearest to November 11, they hold the "Räbenkilbi," a biggish event originally staged in honour of the parish church patron, St. Martin. Nowadays it includes a colourful procession with many floats whose brightly-lit turnips represent different themes.

## 72. Rütlischiessen

The customs associated with shooting in Central Switzerland are connected with the old civilisation of the alpine herdsmen. From alpine hunting developed the art of marksmanship, used with such good effect in the struggles for freedom of the old Confederates, and whose symbolic upholder is the hero William Tell.

The Rütli shooting contest on the Wednesday before November 11—by tradition the historic date of the Oath of the Rütli—has been held since 1862 and attracts to the Rütli more than 500 Central Swiss marksmen and visitors.

## 73. Martinmas Goose

On November 11 Sursee in Canton Lucerne is the only place in Switzerland where the "Martinigans" or Martinmas Goose is still paid public homage. Martinmas, as the day on which interest was due, was once a very important date and the goose was originally a contribution in kind, in prehistoric times probably also a sacrificial animal.

At three o'clock in the afternoon the "Gansabhauet" is staged in front of the Town Hall. In this game, participants are blindfolded and try to bring down with a single sword stroke a dead goose suspended on a wire.

## 74. The Morgarten Festival

In commemoration of the Battle of Morgarten in 1315—when the Confederates defeated an Austrian Army—the public authorities and the clergy on the morning of November 15 make their way in solemn procession with historical groups from Sattel (Schwyz) after a special church service has been held there, to the Pass of Morgarten leading to the Lake of Ägeri. The historical report is read at the Battle Chapel and speeches recall the battle. At the same time, the Morgarten shooting contest takes place by the Battle Memorial, above the Lake of Ägeri.

## 75. Berne's Onion Market

The best-known and most popular of Switzerland's many big autumn markets is Berne's "Zibelemärit" or onion market, held on the fourth Monday in November.

According to tradition, the market right was granted to the people of the district lying between the Lakes of Morat and Neuchâtel in gratitude for the help they gave after the great fire of Berne in 1405. It is a fact that up into the present century, almost all the people selling their vegetables were from this district.

Pride of place in the market, which is held in front of the Federal Palace and in the Bärenplatz is still taken by onions, which can be seen piled up in great heaps and plaited into garlands and strings.

Apart from the market itself there is a wide choice of amusements. Although to most Bernese it is a normal working day, the event is regarded as a festival of the city folk. The young people stream into the centre for an evening of merrymaking, one of the main attractions being a confetti battle in one of the main streets.

For a number of years the masked "Zibelegrinde" figures have been making the round of the restaurants and cafés with their satires on current events.

### 76. St. Nicholas

The figures of St. Nicholas, who on December 6 goes round sometimes dressed like a venerable bishop and sometimes like a bogeyman to frighten the children, and his escorts unite totally different characteristics. The Bishop of Myra in Asia Minor, who rapidly became popular and legendary throughout Europe for his acts of charity and his miraculous deeds, is obviously represented by the saintly figure whose rôle as the children's friend was especially welcome to the medieval church, since it pushed more and more into the background older pagan usages widespread at the beginning of December. But the pre-Christian influences still appear in noise, punishment, and demand for tribute, as well as in the placatory gifts, which are characteristic of St. Nicholas and especially of his satellites. The dual aspect of the custom comes particularly to the fore in Central Switzerland. In some places big noisy processions have become tradition.

Particularly impressive in Küssnacht am Rigi, and also in Arth are these "Klausjagen," given a very special flavour by the so-called "Iffelträger," wearing gigantic headgear illuminated from the inside by candles.

### 77. "Escalade" in Geneva

The "Escalade" festival in Geneva recalls the unsuccessful attack on the city by Savoyard troops on the night of December 11/12, 1602.

A weekend evening is generally selected for the picturesque Proclamation Procession, whose participants, in costumes of the period, march in the flickering light of flaming pitch torches in the streets of the old quarter between Bourg-de-Four and St. Gervais on both sides of the River Rhone. Among them are historical or legendary figures like "Mère Royaume," who poured the boiling contents of her copper cauldron on a Savoyard soldier.

A mounted herald wearing the colours of Geneva announces the success of the alert defenders at several points in the city. A commemorative service is held in St. Pierre's Cathedral.

The Escalade was for a time a kind of substitute for the masquerades abolished by the Reformation; disguised figures known as "Savoyards" disporting themselves and masked balls were also organised. But in recent decades this aspect of the tradition has retreated very much into the background, and the accent has fallen more on the patriotic character of the event.

## 78. "Schnabelgeissen"

Among the "bogeymen," symbolising nightmare figures taken over from pre-Christian beliefs, who roister around at the time of the winter solstice, the "Schnabelgeissen" deserve attention. Dressed in white sheets, they go in for all kinds of pranks with their big wooden beaks: they appear on a Friday shortly before Christmas at Ottenbach (Zurich), generally on December 30 at the "Tricheln" (bell ringing by children) at Oberhasli, Canton Berne, and at the "Haggeri-Jagen" in the neighbourhood of Richterswil on the Lake of Zurich.

## 79. Christmas

In complete contrast to the noise of the traditions with their roots in pagan times, Christmas is a festival of peace and quiet. The day of Christ's birth as the "Light of the World" was originally celebrated on January 6. The Church transferred it intentionally to December 25, superimposing it on more ancient customs which still persisted. The custom of "Sternsingen"—a form of caroling—is really linked to Epiphany. In some places, however, such as in Lucerne and Wettingen (Aarau), it has been brought forward in recent years to shortly before Christmas, and given further artistic embellishment.

## 80. Sebastian Singers at Rheinfelden

Since the Plague Year of 1541, the 12 members of the "Brotherhood of Sebastian" in Rheinfelden have sung by the seven town wells on Christmas Eve just before midnight and again on New Year's Eve.

## 81. "Restauration" in Geneva

With brief ceremonies and artillery salutes on the evening of December 30 and the morning of December 31, Geneva commemorates the "Restauration" of 1813, which for the city brought the Napoleonic era to an end.

## 82. New Year's Eve

Reducing the holy figure of December 6 to a purely daemonic character, groups of "Kläuse" dance and racket on the morning of New Year's Eve or in the evening, to the noise of bells and the crack of whips, and demanding money. In this way they carry on their antics through various East Swiss villages and their surroundings: through Wald and Stäfa (Zurich), Oberschaan in the St. Gall Rhine Valley and through the Appenzell "Hinterland." Primitive noise is also a feature of the "Achetringeler," masked figures who go through the little town of Laupen, Canton Berne, at 8 o'clock on New Year's Eve.

## Traditions And Popular Festivals In Switzerland

| No. | Festival | Where Held | When |
|---|---|---|---|
| 1. | The turn of the year | | January 1 |
| 2. | The "Kläuse" of Appenzell | Commune of Urnäsch | January 13 |
| 3. | "Greiflet" in Schwyz | Schwyz, Brunnen | January 6 |
| 4. | Engadine "Schlitteda" | Upper Engadine | January |
| 5. | The three kings and their star | Beromünster and other Lucerne localities as well as in Grisons and South Ticino | January |
| 6. | Women and girls celebrate in the Seetal | Fahrwangen, Meisterschwanden (Aargau) | 2nd Sunday of New Year |
| 7. | "Vogel Gryff" in Basel | Basel | January 13, 20, or 24 |
| 8. | St. Sebastian at Finhaut | Finhaut (Valais) | January 20 |
| 9. | "Homstrom" at Scuol | Scuol/Schuls | 1st Sunday of February |
| 10. | Carnival customs galore | Basel and West Switzerland | Middle of January to Ash Wednesday |
| 11. | Lötschental "Roitschäggättä" | Villages in Lötschental | Shrove Thursday |
| 12. | Carnival in Canton Schwyz | Schwyz and Einsiedeln | Carnival Monday or Tuesday |
| 13. | Lucerne's "Fritschi" parade | Lucerne | Shrove Thursday |
| 14. | Risotto meal in the Ticino | Bigger localities in the Ticino | Shrove Tuesday |
| 15. | "Greth-Schell" in Zug | Zug | Carnival Monday |
| 16. | Carnival bonfires | Canton Zurich | Sunday after Ash Wednesday |

## Swiss Festivals In North America

| No. | Festival | Where Held | When |
|---|---|---|---|
| 17. | Carnival time in the St. Gall Rhine Valley and Seztal | Flums, Berschis, Walenstadt | Carnival Sunday and Tuesday |
| 18. | "Gidio Hosenstoss" at Herisau | Herisau (Appenzell-Ausserrhoden) | Ash Wednesday |
| 19. | Hurling the disc | Matt (Glarus) | Carnival Sunday |
| 20. | "Lichterschwemmen" | Unterengstringen and Ellikon (ZH) Islikon (TG), Ermensee (LU) | Generally third Sunday before Easter |
| 21. | "Aeschlibuebe" | Elgg (Zurich) | Ash Wednesday |
| 22. | Basel Fasnacht | Basel | Monday to Wednesday following Ash Wednesday |
| 23. | Groppenfasnacht | Ermatingen (Thurgau) | Third Sunday before Easter |
| 24. | Chalanda Marz | Upper Engadine | March 1 |
| 25. | Neuchâtel's constitution | Neuchâtel | March 1 |
| 26. | Palm Sunday observances | Central Switzerland and Catholic cantons of East Switzerland | Palm Sunday |
| 27. | Mendrisio Good Friday processions | Mendrisio | Maundy Thursday and Good Friday |
| 28. | Egg races | Rural Basel and Bözberg district and some localities of Bernese Lake District | Easter Monday or Sunday after Easter |
| 29. | Easter alms | Ferden (Lötschental) | Easter Monday |
| 30. | The Näfels pilgrimage | Näfels (Glarus) | 1st Thursday in April |
| 31. | Zurich's "Sechseläuten" | Zurich | A Monday in April |

| No. | Festival | Where Held | When |
| --- | --- | --- | --- |
| 32. | Landsgemeinden | Appenzell, Unterwalden, Glarus | Last Sunday in April |
| 33. | Singing-in May | Zurich | May 1 |
| 34. | "Mai-Bären" | Bad Ragaz | 1st Sunday in May |
| 35. | "Feuillu" | Canton Geneva | 1st Sunday in May |
| 36. | "Maggiolata" in Ticino | Lugano District | 1st Sunday in May |
| 37. | The Vaudois "Abbayes" | Montreux | May |
| 38. | Stoss pilgrimage | Appenzell | May 14 |
| 39. | Ladies' shooting contest | Entlebuch, Escholzmatt and Schupfheim (Lucerne) | Every three years in May |
| 40. | Ascension Day ride | Beromünster, Sempach, Hitzkirch | Ascension Day |
| 41. | Pacing the bounds in Rural Basel | Liestal | Monday before Ascension Day |
| 42. | Corpus Christi | Many Catholic Districts | 2nd Thursday after Whitsun |
| 43. | Benediction Sunday | Lötschental | Sunday after Corpus Christi |
| 44. | June the first in Geneva | Geneva | June 1, evening |
| 45. | Ascent to summer pastures | Gruyères, Appenzell, etc. | June |
| 46. | Cow fights in Valais | Val d'Hérens and other valleys | June |
| 47. | Battle of Morat commemoration | Morat | June 22 |
| 48. | Children's festivals | Burgdorf, Brugg, Aarau | Last Monday in June and second Thursday and Friday respectively in July |

| No. | Festival | Where Held | When |
|---|---|---|---|
| 49. | St. Gall children's festival | St. Gall | Every two years; end of June and beginning of July |
| 50. | Sempach battle commemoration | Sempach | Monday morning after July |
| 51. | Feast of St. Placidus | Disentis | July 11 |
| 52. | Dornach battle commemoration | Dornach (Solothurn) | Sunday after July 22 |
| 53. | Alp festivals | Bernese Oberland | Midsummer |
| 54. | Alpine religious services | Gastern, near Kandersteg | 1st Sunday in August |
| 55. | "Maria zum Schnee" | Rigi, Meglisalp, Bettmeralp, Schwarzsee near Zermatt | August 5 |
| 56. | "Bergsonntag" | Northern Graubünden | Midsummer |
| 57. | Swiss National Day | Throughout Switzerland | August 1 |
| 58. | "Lüdern-Chilbi" | Emmental | Sunday before or after August 10 |
| 59. | Saignelégier horse market Horse market | Saignelégier, Chaindon (Reconvilier) | 2nd weekend of August; 1st Sunday in September |
| 60. | Shepherds' festivals | Daubensee (near the Gemmi Pass) | 2nd Sunday in August |
| 61. | Blessings on the Alps | Anniviers Valley | Sunday at end of August |
| 62. | Cheese distribution in the Justis Valley | Merlingen and Sigriswil | End of September |
| 63. | "Kilbi" and "Bénichon" | Fribourg | Sundays in September and October |

| No. | Festival | Where Held | When |
|---|---|---|---|
| 64. | "Bachfischet" | Aarau | Beginning of September |
| 65. | "Knabenschiessen" | Zurich | Second weekend in September |
| 66. | "Ausschiesset" | Thun | End of September |
| 67. | "Stecklitragen" | Wil (St. Gall) | 1st or 2nd Sunday in October |
| 68. | Grape harvest festivals | Sierre (Valais), Neuchâtel, Lugano | Last Sunday in September or first Sunday in October |
| 69. | "Lesesonntage" on the Lake of Bienne | Lake of Bienne District | Sundays, mid-September to mid-October |
| 70. | Alpine popular festivals | Obwalden and Nidwalden | End of October or beginning of November |
| 71. | "Räbenlichter" | Canton Zurich | Beginning of November |
| 72. | "Rütlischiessen" | Rütli | Wednesday before November 11 |
| 73. | Martinmas goose | Sursee (Lucerne) | November 11 |
| 74. | Morgarten festival | Morgarten | November 15 |
| 75. | Berne's onion market | Berne | 4th Monday in November |
| 76. | St. Nicholas | Küssnacht am Rigi, Arth | Around December 5 |
| 77. | Escalade | Geneva | Around December 11/12 |
| 78. | "Schnabelgeissen" | Ottenbach (ZH) | Shortly before Christmas |

| No. | Festival | Where Held | When |
|---|---|---|---|
| 79. | Christmas | | December 25 |
| 80. | Sebastian singers | Rheinfelden | Christmas Eve just before midnight, and New Year's Eve |
| 81. | "Restauration" | Geneva | December 30-31 |
| 82. | New Year's Eve | Wald (ZH), Stäfa (ZH), Oberschaan (SG) | December 31 |

# Sports, Games, and Recreation

## Historical Background

The structure of sport and its specifically Swiss characteristics can be understood only in the light of the history of this small country in the heart of Europe. For long periods of time, "in the heart of Europe" meant being surrounded by the stress and tensions of larger Powers, frequently in conflict, in the danger zone of their wars.

The freedom and independence of what was to be the Confederation were gained and defended through resort to arms. Defending it has meant being ever ready for war. Hence, for Swiss citizens, wielding arms has ever been an everyday thing, and the weapon became the symbol of freedom. A seal on a document from Lucerne, dated 1235, shows the first known representation of the crossbow, a weapon which was to play an important role for many years. There are many indications that already in the fourteenth century practice in shooting was regulated by official decree in many cantons and cities. The second part of the century brought gunpowder and guns. Around 1500 the crossbow was abandoned as a wartime weapon; as an instrument of sport it has remained in favour.

Far back in history we find proof of other sportive activities. First and foremost was wrestling. We detect two wrestlers among the carved figures of the thirteenth century choir stalls in the Cathedral of Lausanne. A historical document from the year 1508 represents public games in Einsiedeln, featuring wrestling, running, stone-putting, and a longjump. We have a warning from Ulrich Zwingli, the reformer, which admonished wrestlers as far back as 1526 that they should restrain themselves lest competition degenerate into serious fighting. A variation of wrestling called *Schwingen* (Swiss wrestling) came into vogue in the sixteenth century and is still very popular with the Alpine herdsmen of central Switzerland and the Bernese *Oberland*.

Along with wrestling, Swiss wrestling, running, stone-putting, the longjump, and shooting with the crossbow (and later with guns), strangely enough even swimming played an important role among the exercises of that time, particularly of course in towns and places along the lakes and rivers. In 1525, the authorities of Zurich found it necessary to take measures against the noise and other excesses resulting from jumping off bridges and waterwheels along the Limmat, which would indicate that the youth of that time were very familiar with the water. Indeed, quite early the boys aged between eight and fifteen were grouped into youth teams and trained in shooting and other sports. In the seventeenth century, shooting practice was compulsory for the boys of Zurich. No doubt, today's popular *Knabenschiessen* (shooting competitions for boys) goes back to this flourishing shooting sport in old Zurich.

## SCHWINGEN (SWISS WRESTLING)

*Schwingen* is probably as old as Switzerland itself and originated as a pastime of the cowherds in the Alps. Its popularity as a game of combat was known to have existed from the sixteenth century. Its participants consider Swiss wrestling not so much a sport as a game with a folkloristic tradition. As the name suggests, the goal is to throw the opponent to the ground within a large sawdust ring using a swinging motion and, either directly or with further efforts on the ground, force one's opponent onto his back. The various ways of doing this all have names in German.

*Left: Swiss wrestling: taking hold of the opponent. Right: Swiss wrestling: the round is under way. Credit: Swiss National Tourist Office.*

The combatants pull a pair of short, leather-belted cotton or linen trunks over their ordinary long trousers or gymnastics trousers. Before the contest begins, each takes hold of his opponent in a prescribed manner; the right hand grabs the top of the opponent's wrestling trunks in the small of his back; the left grabs the turned-up seam on the right leg. When the umpire calls out *Gut* ("good") the round or *Gang* begins. The duration, between five and ten minutes for the round, is determined in advance by the jury in accordance with the occasion and the participation. The contest is decided when one of the two wrestlers touches the sawdust-padded ground with both shoulder blades, provided that his opponent holds him down in that position for three seconds. (The winner always brushes the sawdust off his opponent. This is a traditional gesture to show that there are no hard feelings.) If both wrestlers prove equally strong, and neither is the victor, the round is stopped (*gestellt*) and is considered as a draw. In this case between eight and nine points are given to each. If the victory is clear, the winner receives at least nine and, at best, the maximum of ten points. The loser gets between 7.5 and 8.75 points. There is no classification by weight. The jury arranges the participants into pairs of opponents with approximately matching physique and ability in wrestling. All contestants take part in the *Anschwingen* with a first and second round and in the *Ausschwingen*, i.e. the third and fourth rounds. Only 40 to 60 percent can take part in the *Ausstich*, the decisive fifth and sixth rounds.

A distinction can be made between *Sennenschwinger* (herdsmen wrestlers) and *Turnerschwinger* (gymnasts). The former are dressed in a shirt and ordinary dark trousers, the latter in a short-sleeved white sweatshirt and long white trousers. This classification does not imply that every herdsman-wrestler earns his living on the alpine meadows. But it does mean that he belongs to a herdsmen's Swiss wrestling club, while the others belong to a gymnastics club.

Today, *Schwingen* is the only sports activity where there is no publicity material anywhere on the field. Even being looked after by a masseur or physiotherapist at the ringside was taboo until recently. However, changing times have turned these highly popular events into high-performance sports, with participants who have been trained accordingly, not least because the prizes to be won are very valuable. In the spirit of what was originally a peasants' game, the winner usually receives a young bull (sometimes a heifer), for the runners-up, valuable products of the cabinet maker are offered, such as chests and tables, and other prizes always include large cowbells. Cash is never offered as a prize (that would offend the spirit of the games), but the winner of a bull can usually find a buyer for it, even before leaving the arena.

The climax is the national festival of *Schwingen*, which takes place every three years and lasts two days, the only time the entire wrestling elite of the country competes together. Apart from this, competitions are held only at the cantonal level or within the four member associations. Sometimes a few *Schwinger* guests (leading competitors from other regions) are invited to these meets.

The scoring system for *Schwingen* is worthy of special attention. What at first appears to be old-fashioned and unfair is in fact a brilliant method and could be taken as a model for other kinds of sport that suffer from a decline in spectators because they are insufficiently attractive. A normal competition has five rounds, which means that each participant competes five times against different opponents. The pairs are not chosen by lot, but are determined by the committee, so that in the first round, the expected strongest and second strongest fight against each other, then numbers three, four, five, and six, and so on. Then the pairings are made on the basis of the first round results, the leader against the second, and so on. During the course of the day, the intermediate standings give a misleading picture of the relative strengths, but this is gradually corrected after each round, and at the end, the best competitors are at the head of the table. A number of attractive duels have been seen, and the last round produces a real final; there is no chance winner through fortunate seedings. The second stroke of genius is the scoring for each round. Not every victory is worth the same. Depending on the clarity, attractiveness, and offensive spirit shown, a win may bring 9.25 to 10 points, a drawn match 8.25 to 9, and a defeat 8 to 8.75. It cannot be denied that there are of course often discussions among the spectators about the points awarded by the all-powerful jury. The national champion (*Schwingerkönig*) enjoys high prestige during his three-year reign, and in individual communities a lot of respect is accorded even to one who has won a laurel wreath for a place in the first third of the field.

## HORNUSSEN (HORNETS)

From descriptions in 1840 by the Swiss novelist Jeremias Gotthelf, we know that even at that time *Hornussen* was the favorite game of Bernese countryfolk. The game is still popular today, particularly in the

*Left: Hornussen: the Hornuss is mounted on the batting stock and in a moment will be on its way to the Ries. Credit: Swiss National Tourist Office.*

Bernese Emmental and Middle Land, but also in the countryside of neighboring cantons. A Swiss association founded in 1902 is in charge. It maintains close partnership with the Association of Swiss Wrestlers. The game is played on flat fields recently harvested. The area is about 300 meters (984 feet) long and about 30 meters (98 feet) wide. The playing field, when staked out, looks like a wedged piece of pie. At its point stands the batting stock. Teams take turns against each other alternately, as hitters or as catchers. From the batting stock to a distance of 100 meters (328 feet) is the "zero" zone into which fall the badly hit *"Hornusse."* The valid "zone," or *"Ries,"* starts at 100 meters. Its normal dimensions are a width of seven meters (23 feet) at the 100 meters mark and of eleven meters (36 feet) at the 270 meter distance. The *"Ries"* itself is therefore 170 meters (558 feet) long. Within that zone the party of catchers, or *"Abtuer"* spreads out, armed with catching boards called *"Schindeln"* in their hands which they throw up at the right moment to stop the flight of the *"nouss"* or *"hornuss."*

The *"hornuss"* is appropriately named after the dreaded insect, the hornet. In flying through the air, the *"hornuss"* generates a humming sound

*Left: Hornussen: the Abtuer are in action. The Hornuss can be seen in flight. A number of spectators are to the rear.* Credit: Swiss National Tourist Office.

that resembles somewhat the buzz of a hornet (*"hornis"*)—hence the name. The *"hornuss"* has the shape of a small puck, 60 millimeters (about 2 1/2 inches) in diameter and 3.1 centimeters (about 1 1/4 inches) thick. It weighs about 76 grams (about 2 1/2 ounces). It is poised on a small ball of clay atop the batting stock at the upper end of a slanting guiding rail 220 centimeters (about 7 feet) long. The batting is done with the *"stecken,"* a whip-like rod more than two meters (6 1/2 feet) long with a flexible handle and fitted at its point with a rounded wooden hitting device (*"träf"*). The batter swings the *"stecken"* around his body before whipping it along the slanting rail to hit the *"nouss"* from the stock.

To be good as to distance and direction, a drive demands both strength and precision. Each member of the batting party (16 men) is entitled to three attempts to strike the *"Hornuss."* The batsman forfeits his right to bat if his *Hornuss* is knocked down by the other party within the *Ries*. The opposing party therefore tries to knock down the *Hornuss* as soon as possible. The *Schindeln* are held up high or even thrown up. This catching or *Abtun* takes a good eye and sense of distance. There are only fractions of a second in which to see, estimate, run, jump, and throw up the board.

If the *Hornuss* lands within the *Ries* without having been touched by a *Schindel*, this counts as a point. The score for a team is the total of the distances reached, measured not in meters but in "fields," sixteen to eighteen of which make up the *Ries*. The worst result is if the *Nouss* falls to the ground without having been hit by a single *Schindel*. The team in the field then receives a *Numero* or minus point, and has no chance of winning, since the decision goes first according to these *Numeros* and only if there are none, according to the total length reached. The speed of the *Nouss* has been measured at almost 300 kilometers per hour (almost 190 miles per hour), and it has been known to reach a distance of more than 300 meters (328 yards)! As with *Schwingen*, there is a national competition every three years at which a champion is selected, the best individual player, the outstanding hitter. Apart from Switzerland, *Hornussen* is practiced only by a few people in South Africa, who call it "Helvetian golf." More recently, this sport, which traces its origins to medieval war games, when hands and stones were used instead of power and guns, has found some interest in Germany. In Switzerland, there are over six thousand active players.

## Military Cross Country (Waffenlauf)

The *Waffenlauf* is a sport practiced only in Switzerland. The special feature of these long-distance runs of 18 to 42 kilometers (11 to 19 miles) on roads and country paths is that the competitor runs in full military uniform, including a backpack and rifle weighing 7.5 kilograms (16 1/2 pounds). This burden produces a typical, rather heavy stride. Originally, army boots were obligatory, then black shoes were allowed, and in recent years, the choice of footwear is free, and a lot of bright colors now stand out from the uniform. There are eleven races per year, always over the same courses, finishing with the Frauenfeld race over the marathon distance of 42.2 kilometers (26 miles), the longest by far. A few years ago one thousand and more participants were normal, but the rising popularity of jogging, with races for the general public, has produced a lot of competition, and the number of participants has fallen to between five hundred and nine hundred at present.

## The Federal Shoot

Once a year the (voluntary) Federal Shoot takes place. On this weekend, at every shooting range in Switzerland, those with rifles fire

*Left: Swiss wrestling: taking hold of the opponent. Right: Swiss wrestling: the round is under way. Credit: Swiss National Tourist Office.*

their eighteen rounds at 300 meters (984 feet) and those with pistols at 25 or 50 meters (82 or 164 feet). More than two hundred thousand people take part, which regularly prompts the media to use the headline "Greatest Sporting Event in the World"!

## STEINTOSSEN (STONE THROWING)

The date of the first *Steintossen* festival was held at Unspunnen in 1805, hence the name, the Unspunnen Stone. This granite boulder weighs 83 kilograms (185 pounds). The record in recent years is a little more than 3 meters (about 10 feet).

# Discovering The Music Of Switzerland

## Folk and "Evergreen" Music

As an introduction to Swiss music, you might try *Hello Switzerland*, produced by Tell Recordings. It has medleys performed by Swiss folklore choruses and yodeling duets, as well as selections of alphenhorn festival music. The alphenhorn is a wind instrument that, whether straight or curved into a more efficient spiral, can measure up to 14 feet in length. The album *20 Beliebte Melodien* (20 Beloved Melodies), issued by Helvetia Recordings, contains some of Switzerland's more popular folk songs interpreted by yodeling masters. Runedi Rymann, Switzerland's greatest yodeler, has an album of his own, *Das Komponisten-Portrait Ruedi Rymann* (Activ Recordings), offering 16 examples of his superior artistry. For those wishing a little more oompha, there is *Zoge am Boge im Heugade Obe*, compiled by Activ Recordings.

No one interested in Swiss folk tunes should omit the country's *Handorgan* (accordian) music. An excellent representation is offered by the Käslin Brothers' Handorgan Duet, whose popular foot-twitching melodies—*schottisch* (melodies to accompany a singing trio) and *Ländler* (melodies for a small band)—are recorded on Phonoplay's *Käslin & Käslin*. Among the selections are "Mirabella Fox" and "Ballantine-Whisky Time."

## Popular

One group whose music carefully mingles the big-band and the Swiss evergreen traditions is the Geschwister Schmid Band, whose "oldies" album *Grüezi, Grüezi* (produced by Gold Records) is played at reunions and ballrooms across the country. More international in scope is an album called *Dixie-Ländler* by the PS Corporation Engadiner Landlerfründa; it charmingly mixes Swiss evergreen music with Dixieland jazz.

## CLASSICAL

The classical tradition in Switzerland has borrowed so heavily from the musical traditions in neighboring countries that it has few exponents of a genuinely Swiss idiom. A notable exception is composer Arthur Honegger—and even he is claimed jointly by the French. His grand and somber choral work, *King David* (composed in 1921), is available in versions recorded by the Orchestre de la Suisse Romande (London Records) and by the Friburg Collegium Musicum (Christophorus Records).

## ALPHORN

On the other hand, an excellent compilation of Swiss alphenhorn music is available from Clavex Records, *In Praise of the Alphorn*. It contains 16 pieces by several artists. Another album is *Cor des Alpes/ Alphorn* (Disques Office), which contains a sampling of melodies from the past 200 years of Swiss musical tradition.

# SCHERENSCHNITT

© Ursula Kaeshammer Alther

On the opposite page is a *scherenschnitt* especially designed for this book. The artist, Ursula Kaeshammer Alther, describes her creation as follows:

In the center, I put a heart decorated with flowers to reflect our love for our old *Heimat* (homeland). Around the heart, I arranged the most typical Swiss *Brauche* (customs):

- an alphornblower
- two swingers
- a dancing girl
- a flag thrower

All this activity is surrounded in a circle by an *Alpaufzug* (procession of the cattle to and from the Alps). In the top right corner is seen the Matterhorn, one of the most characteristic mountains of Switzerland.

As for the *Auslandschweizer* (Swiss living outside Switzerland), they are like the vines, growing in and out of the outer circle which represents the Swiss borders. They find their way wherever they go, always keeping a bond with the old country.

*Ursula Kaeshammer Alther*

## THE FLAG OF SWITZERLAND

The Swiss flag is red with a white couped cross which recalls the time of the crusades. The Swiss cantons of Uri, Schwyz, and Unterwalden, after joining in the "eternal union" in 1291, did indeed use a simple red flag as their campaigning colours. In 1339, however, by which time Lucerne had also joined the confederation, a white cross on red was adopted as a common sign in the struggle for freedom against the Habsburgs, because "freedom of their own people was just as sacred as the deliverance of the Holy Land." There was also, however, a connection with medieval imperial symbolism in which the colours red and white and the cross played a great role.

The Swiss have thus shown their loyalty to the Holy Roman Empire, while refusing any indirect subservience to any feudal lord. The red flag of Schwyz of 1240 was probably taken as the model and in 1289 Rudolf I of Germany added a white cross to commemorate the help of Swiss mercenaries against the Czechs. In 1815, this flag was expressly confirmed by an order of General Bachmann, and in 1848, it was declared to be the confederation flag. Its present form was defined in 1889; it is square and the length of each arm of the cross is one-sixth greater than its width. Since 1941, the merchant flag has been a rectangular version of the national flag with the proportions 2:3.

## Area and Population

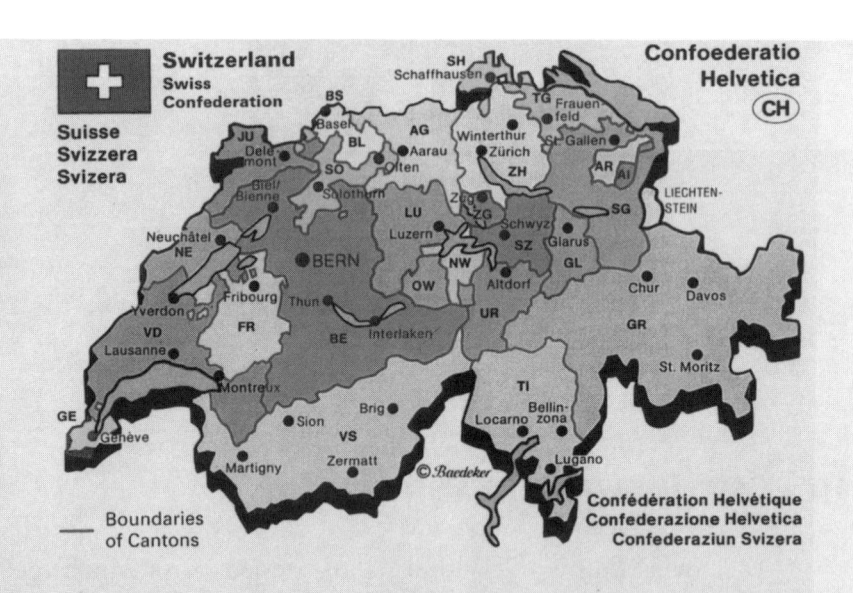

| Cantons | Area in sq. km (sq. miles) | Population (1991) | Cantons | Area in sq. km (sq. miles) | Population (1991) |
| --- | --- | --- | --- | --- | --- |
| AG Aargau | 1405 (542) | 496,200 | Unterwalden: | | |
| AR Appenzell-Ausserrhoden | 243 (94) | 51,400 | NW Nidwalden | 276 (107) | 32,600 |
| | | | OW Obwalden | 491 (190) | 28,800 |
| AI Appenzell-Innerrhoden | 172 (66) | 13,500 | SG St Gallen | 2014 (778) | 420,200 |
| | | | SH Schaffhausen | 298 (115) | 71,600 |
| BL Basel-Land | 428 (165) | 230,100 | SZ Schwyz | 908 (351) | 110,500 |
| BS Basel-Stadt | 37 (14) | 191,700 | SO Solothurn | 791 (305) | 226,600 |
| BE Berne | 6050 (2335) | 945,500 | TG Thurgau | 1013 (391) | 205,900 |
| FR Fribourg | 1670 (645) | 207,700 | TI Ticino | 2811 (1085) | 286,700 |
| GE Geneva | 282 (109) | 375,900 | UR Uri | 1076 (415) | 33,600 |
| GL Glarus | 685 (264) | 37,600 | VS Valais | 5226 (2018) | 248,300 |
| GR Grisons | 7106 (2744) | 170,400 | VD Vaud | 3219 (1243) | 583,600 |
| JU Jura | 837 (323) | 65,600 | ZG Zug | 239 (92) | 84,900 |
| LU Lucerne | 1492 (576) | 319,500 | ZH Zurich | 1729 (668) | 1,150,500 |
| NE Neuchâtel | 797 (308) | 160,600 | CH Swiss Confederation | 41,293 (15,943) | 6,750,600 |

## The Cantons of the Swiss Confederation

**Aargau (AG)**
Canton since 1803
Capital: Aarau

**Appenzell-Ausserrhoden (AR)**
Half-canton since 1513
Capital: Herisau

**Appenzell-Innerrhoden (AI)**
Half-canton since 1513
Capital: Appenzell

**Basel-Land (BL)**
Half-canton since 1501
Capital: Liestal

**Basel-Stadt (BS)**
Half-canton since 1501
Capital: Basle

**Berne (BE)**
Canton since 1353
Capital: Berne

**Fribourg (FR)**
Canton since 1481
Capital: Fribourg

**Geneva (GE)**
Canton since 1815
Capital: Geneva

**Glarus (GL)**
Canton since 1352
Capital: Glarus

**Grisons (GR)**
Canton since 1803
Capital: Chur

**Jura (JU)**
Canton since 1979
Capital: Delémont

**Lucerne (LU)**
Canton since 1332
Capital: Lucerne

**Neuchâtel (NE)**
Canton since 1815
Capital: Neuchâtel

**Nidwalden (NW)**
Half-canton since 1291
Capital: Stans

**Obwalden (OW)**
Half-canton since 1291
Capital: Sarnen

**St Gallen (SG)**
Canton since 1803
Capital: St Gallen

**Schaffhausen (SH)**
Canton since 1501
Capital: Schaffhausen

**Schwyz (SZ)**
Canton since 1291
Capital: Schwyz

**Solothurn (SO)**
Canton since 1481
Capital: Solothurn

**Thurgau (TG)**
Canton since 1803
Capital: Frauenfeld

**Ticino (TI)**
Canton since 1803
Capital: Bellinzona

**Uri (UR)**
Canton since 1291
Capital: Altdorf

**Valais (VS)**
Canton since 1815
Capital: Sion

**Vaud (VD)**
Canton since 1803
Capital: Lausanne

**Zug (ZG)**
Canton since 1352
Capital: Zug

**Zurich (ZH)**
Canton since 1351
Capital: Zurich

Unterwalden

# NORTH AMERICAN SWISS FESTIVALS

*Edmonton, Alberta*

## NORTH AMERICAN SWISS SINGING FESTIVAL

*Description:* Every three years in different locations, the many Swiss singing societies in the U.S.A. and Canada gather together for fun and fellowship over a four-day period to perform original Swiss music in all four Swiss languages. Friendly competition, sightseeing, and a Grand Concert in full costume make for a memorable event. The North American Swiss Singing Alliance was founded in 1896 as the Schweizer-Amerikanischer Sängerbund (Swiss American Singing Alliance) by representatives from Toledo, Cleveland, Columbus, and Sandusky, Ohio, and Pittsburgh, Pennsylvania.

*Location:* Winspear Centre For Music

*Date of festival:* Every three years, usually in late June or early July. In 2000, the festival will be held in Edmonton from Thursday evening, June 29, through Sunday, July 2; festival will be held in the U.S.A. in 2003.

*Year first conducted:* 1897

*Last year's attendance:* 600

*For more information, contact:*
   Karl A. Hirzel, Jr., President
   North American Swiss Singing Alliance
   5405 Hanley Road
   Walbridge, OH 43465
   Telephone: (419) 837-5042

*What to explore nearby:* Edmonton is a wonderful summer destination with about seventeen hours of sunlight in the summer solstice, miles of river valley parkland, and friendly citizens. Swiss Festival 2000 will take place in the heart of the city within easy walking distance to hotels and shopping. Visit the extensive West Edmonton Mall. Also, within easy reach of Edmonton by road, you will find Elk Island National Park where you may get up close and personal with buffalo, elk, deer, and a myriad of other wildlife. Nearby Beaverhills Lake is not only home to an amazing number of waterfowl, but is also a major stopover for migrating birds on the major flyway that runs through Alberta. Jasper and the Rocky Mountains are three and a half hours by road to the west. A post Festival tour through Jasper, Lake Louise, Banff, and Calgary will provide not only spectacular scenery, but also an opportunity to attend the world-famous Calgary Stampede.

# Coquitlam, British Columbia

### SCHÜTZENFEST
(NEAR VANCOUVER)

*Description:* The annual "Schützenfest" features two full days of target shooting with categories for juniors, ladies, as well as for men. Ranges include one for full-bore, pistol, small bore, crossbow, and trap. You can enjoy lunch and dinner on both days. On Sunday evening, join the festivities for the much-anticipated *absenden* (awards presentation). We have enjoyed friendly competitions from our neighbors in Alberta, Washington state, and California. Our chalet is always brimming with excitement and fun for all.

*Location:* Swiss Canadian Mountain Range Chalet, 4141 Quarry Road, Burke Mountain, Coquitlam, BC  V3C 3V4

*Date of festival:* Second weekend in October

*Admission fee:* No admission fee; full shooting program is about $40; individual program available for less

*Hours of festival:* from 9:00 a.m. on Saturday to 12:00 midnight on Sunday

*Year first conducted:* 1982

*Last year's attendance:* 200

*Directions:* Coquitlam is located thirty miles northeast of downtown Vancouver. See the upper right of the schematic map.

*For more information, contact:*
    Roy Schürmann
    Swiss Canadian Mountain Range Association
    2120 A Smithline Road
    Abbotsford, BC  V3G 1Y6
    Telephone: (604) 853-0718

*What to explore nearby:* While in the area, take time to visit English Bay in Stanley Park or ride the gondola to the top of Grouse Mountain for a breathtaking view of Vancouver. For a longer trip, take the two-hour drive north to Whistler along the scenic "sea-to-sky" highway. Fort Langley is an old Hudson Bay fur trading post along the Fraser River.

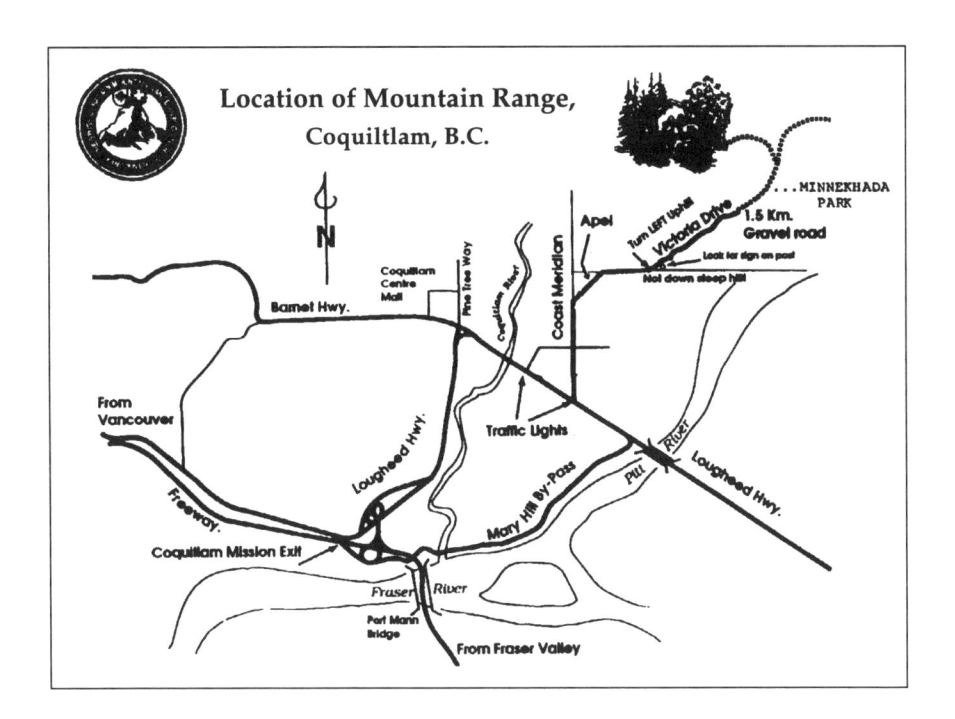

# Toronto, Ontario

## SWISS THEATRE EVENING

*Description:* The annual performance by the Toronto Swiss Theatre Group offers an evening of enjoyable entertainment.

*Location:* Estonian House, 958 Broadview Avenue (near Bloor and Danford)

*Date of festival:* March/April

*Admission fee:* $10

*Hours of festival:* Performance is two hours long, presented twice in Toronto (additional performances are given in Ottawa and Mitchell)

*Year first conducted:* 1973

*Last year's attendance:* 1000

*Directions:* Follow Yonge north to Bloor, then east to Danford, to 958 Broadview Avenue.

*For more information, contact:*
    André A. Farrer, President
    Swiss Club Toronto

2103 Berwick Drive, #22
Burlington, ON L7M 4B7
Telephone: (905) 319-0539

*About Toronto, Ontario:* Toronto is easily accessible—only a one-hour drive away for about five million Canadians and within a comfortable ninety-minute flight to Toronto's International Airport for nearly sixty percent of the U.S. population. In 1989, the United Nations described Toronto as one of the world's most multicultural cities. Its population of 2.3 million includes more than eighty different ethnic groups speaking fifty-two different languages. Toronto has an abundance of green spaces. The city boasts close to 10,000 acres of parkland, beaches, the spectacular Scarborough Bluffs and the unspoiled Toronto Island, a short ferry ride across Toronto Harbour.

*What to explore nearby:* Niagara Falls and the Muskokas

# Rockwood, Ontario

## NATIONAL DAY CELEBRATION

*Description:* The Swiss Club Toronto in cooperation with Hubert Bielmann, chef and owner of La Vieille Auberge Restaurant, in Rockwood, Ontario, invites you to come out and enjoy a great day in the country featuring ensemble folklorique "La Colombiére de Genéve." Come at noon; explore the grounds; taste the food, wine, and beer; and enjoy a coffee *schnaps*. At about 2:00 p.m., the National Day Celebration will begin with an official welcome, convocation, and singing of the national anthem. Following this, there will be a concert by the folklore ensemble and then games. Bring your own chairs. Parking is available in the village centre with attendants.

*Location:* Hubert Bielmann's grounds in Rockwood, Ontario (near Acton)

*Date of festival:* Sunday nearest August 1

*Admission fee:* $5 (includes August 1 badge); children under age 12 are admitted free

*Hours of festival:* Noon until about 8:00 p.m.

*Year first conducted:* 1918

*Last year's attendance:* 1000

*Directions:* On arrival in Rockwood, follow the Swiss flags.

*For more information, contact:*
    André A. Farrer, President
    Swiss Club Toronto
    2103 Berwick Drive, #22
    Burlington, ON L7M 4B7
    Telephone: (905) 319-0539

*What to explore nearby:* Should you wish to make it a weekend, the Rockwood Conservation Park is within walking distance of the grounds and offers swimming, boating, hiking, etc.

# Newark, California

## SPRING AND FALL SCHWINGFESTS

*Description:* The festival features a day-long competition of the Swiss Alpine sports of *Schwingen* (Swiss wrestling) and *Steinstossen* (rock tossing). A Bratwurst or *Schueblig* (Swiss-style sausage) lunch is available from noon to 2:00 p.m. and a barbecued steak is served at 6:00 p.m. The evening program features Swiss Folkmusic by the Kapelle Saelta Nuechter with Frank Beeler on the clarinet followed by Ron Scheiber's Swiss Orchestra. The awarding of crowns, medals, and ribbons to Schwingers and Steinstossers is held in the early evening and dancing to Swiss *volkstuemlicher* music follows.

*Location:* Swiss Park, 5911 Mowry Avenue, Newark, California

*Date of festival:* Spring Schwingfest is held on the last Saturday of May or the first Saturday in June. The Fall Schwingfest is held on the last Saturday in August or on Labor Day weekend, except every three years when a Grand Fall Schwingfest is held.

*Admission fee:* $8

*Hours of festival:* Schwinger registration starts at 8:30 a.m. with wrestling starting at 9:00 a.m.; dancing continues until midnight.

*Year first conducted:* 1928

*Last year's attendance:* 800

*Directions:* The Newark Swiss Park is located at 5911 Mowry Avenue, Newark, California, about ten miles north of San Jose and about forty-five miles southeast of the San Francisco/Oakland area. It is minutes from the Interstate Freeway 880 linking San Jose and Oakland. From San Francisco, take Highway 101 to the San Mateo Bridge (Highway 92) to Highway 880. From all points once on Highway 880, exit at the Mowry Avenue/West turnoff. Travel one-quarter mile further and turn right on Alpenrose Court to the entrance of the Swiss Park. The park consists of a large banquet hall and a large shaded picnic area. Free parking is available.

*For more information, contact:*
    Mariette Franke
    407 Greenwood Drive
    Santa Clara, CA 95054-2134
    Telephone: (408) 988-4351

## First of August Celebration

*Description:* The United Swiss Societies of Northern California organizes the First of August Celebration so that all Swiss and friends of Switzerland can come together to share in the celebrations of Swiss Independence. Great food is prepared and available at the Swiss Park, or you can bring your own picnic. Your entrance fee provides the opportunity to win a great door prize. Kids' games, a Wheel of Fortune, and raffle prizes for all. Enjoy the entertainment (usually music and dancing) throughout the day. Spend the day enjoying the various events.

*Location:* Swiss Park, 5911 Mowry Avenue, Newark, California

*Date of festival:* Sunday nearest August 1

*Admission fee:* About $4, children under age 12 are admitted free

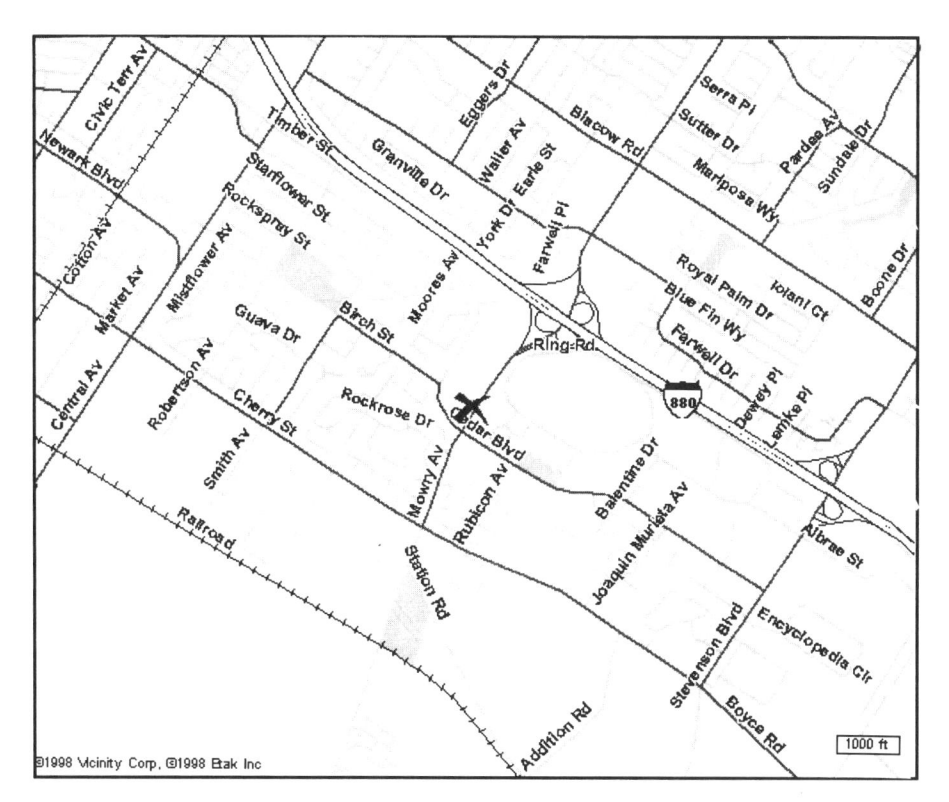

*Swiss Park, 5911 Mowry Avenue, Newark, California*

*Hours of festival:* 11:00 a.m. to 6:00 p.m.

*Year first conducted:* 1912

*Last year's attendance:* 1000

*About Newark:* The city of Newark, California, was a farming community until the early 1950s with many Swiss families operating dairies and farms in the area. On September 21, 1925, the Swiss organized under the name of "Aelpler Gruppe" with the objective to uphold and further Swiss customs and traditions. The name "Aelpler Gruppe" was derived from the Aelpler costumes worn at the Diamond Jubilee parade in San Francisco in 1924. In 1933, property was purchased for a park and banquet hall. Dedication of the hall was on April 7, 1935. Over the years, the Aelpler Gruppe has sponsored biannual Schwingfests, also musicfests, dances, and picnics. The Swiss Park is used annually by the United Swiss Societies of Northern California for their August First Celebration. The ball and picnic grounds are also used by other community organizations for their enjoyment.

*For more information, contact:*
    Rebecca Achermann, Secretary
    United Swiss Societies of Northern California, Inc.
    857 Farley Street
    Mt. View, CA 94043
    Telephone: (650) 964-6875

*What to explore nearby:* There is much to see and do in the Bay area including beautiful oean coastal rocks, the Redwoods, "Great America" (Santa Clara), shopping outlets in Gilroy, and the Great Mall in Milditas, local wineries, and Napa Valley. There is a large shopping center across from the Swiss Park. Newark is located less than one hour's drive from the cities of Oakland, San Francisco, and San Jose. All cities have many points of interest, such as the Golden Gate Bridge, China Town, and cable cars in San Francisco.

# Palo Alto, California

## FIRST OF AUGUST FEST

*Description:* The Peninsula Swiss Club is a friendly organization with the purpose of uniting Swiss people, families, and friends for social gatherings. We celebrate our Swiss heritage and love to share with all people, from all countries, our rich culture and wonderful music. This festival features dining and dancing to the Edelweiss Trio.

*Location:* (see contact person)

*Date of festival:* Weekend nearest August 1

*Admission fee:* About $15

*Hours of festival:* 1:00 p.m. until late evening

*Year first conducted:* 1961

*Last year's attendance:* 150

*For more information, contact:*
    Denise Sanders
    Peninsula Swiss Club
    604 Materdero Avenue
    Palo Alto, CA 94306
    Telephone: (415) 856-4797

## METZGETE

*Description:* This Metzgete is a feast consisting of blood liver sausage followed by dancing.

*Location:* (see contact person)

*Date of festival:* Middle of November

*Admission fee:* About $15

*Hours of festival:* 6:00 p.m. until late evening

*Year first conducted:* 1961

*Last year's attendance:* 150

*For more information, contact:*
    Denise Sanders
    Peninsula Swiss Club
    604 Materdero Avenue
    Palo Alto, CA 94306
    Telephone: (415) 856-4797

# Ripon, California

## SCHWINGFEST AND MUSIKFEST

*Description:* Each year the San Joaquin Valley Swiss Club is host to the Champion Schwingfest conducted by the West Coast Swiss Wrestling Association. The annual meeting of this Association is held in the morning followed by registration of the wrestlers with competitions starting about 11:30 a.m. During the wrestling events, the kitchen and bar are open with musical entertainment. There is also a *steinstossen* competition. After the Schwingfest, a barbeque dinner is served followed by dancing at 7:30 p.m. The awarding of Schwingfest prizes begins about 10:00 p.m. The Musikfest (which is held on a periodic basis) starts with performances by Swiss singers from Washington, Oregon, and California. After the Musikfest ends (about 5:30 p.m.), a barbeque dinner is served followed with dancing beginning at 7:30 p.m.

*Location:* San Joaquin Valley Swiss Club—corner of East Main Street and Manley Road, Ripon, California

*Date of festival:* Last Saturday and Sunday of August

*Admission fee:* $8 per day for adults and $4 for children under age twelve

*Hours of festival:* Schwingfest is on Saturday from 9:00 a.m. to 11:00 p.m. and the Musikfest is on Sunday from 1:00 p.m. to 9:00 p.m.

*Year first conducted:* 1941

*Last year's attendance:* 1000

*About Ripon:* The San Joaquin Valley Swiss Club was founded in 1926 with sixteen Swiss-German members. In 1938, the property was purchased in Ripon. Soon after construction of the hall, an adjoining bar was completed and celebrated by a dedication ceremony in 1941. Since then, the adjoining land purchases and building additions have made this into a fine facility. During its seventy-plus years of existence, membership has grown to 500 members. Events conducted by the Club include three schwingfests each year (one in July for boys only), two concerts and dance, two Swiss parties, barbeques and potlucks.

The stated purpose of San Joaquin Valley Swiss Club is to unite and strengthen the social and patriotic realtions of the Swiss people, Swiss descendants, and their supportive friends in order to encourage, promote, and preserve the culture and traditions of Switzerland.

*For more information, contact:*
   Theresa Beeler, Secretary
   San Joaquin Valley Swiss Club, Inc.
   P. O. Box 373
   Ripon, CA 95366
   Telephone: (209) 599-7267

# Sebastopol, California

## First Augustfeier

*Location:* (see contact person)

*Date of festival:* Nearest Saturday after August 1

*Admission fee:* None (bring a potluck)

*Hours of festival:* 1:00 p.m. to 9:00 p.m.

*Year first conducted:* 1988

*Last year's attendance:* 100

*For more information, contact:*
    Ursula Baur
    The Swiss of Sonoma County
    6700 Orchard Station Road
    Sebastopol, CA 95472
    Telephone: (707) 795-1647 or (707) 829-0235

# Whittier, California

## Swiss Fair
## (Swiss Independence Day Celebration)

*Description:* This August first celebration features a variety of traditional Swiss activities in addition to some modern day "New World" events. Come and enjoy children's games, crossbow shooting, a soccer kick contest, welcoming speech and greetings by a member of the Consulate staff, western line dancing, a children's lampion and flag parade. See performances of alphorn playing, *talerschwingen*, accordion playing, yodeling, a visiting Swiss Harmony Band, Swiss Singing Society. Throughout the day special Swiss foods will be available. A large tent is provided with lots of shade. There are numerous tables of Swiss items for display and sale. Enjoy an evening concert followed by a steak dinner and socializing. (Notice: No food or drinks are to be brought into the park.)

*Location:* Swiss Park Banquet Center, 1905 Workman Mill Road, Whittier, California

*Date of festival:* Sunday closest to August 1

*Admission fee:* $3, children 16 and under are admitted free

*Hours of festival:* 11:00 a.m. to 9:00 p.m.

*Year first conducted:* 1992

*Last year's attendance:* 2000

*Directions:* Whittier is located about twenty minutes north of Disneyland and about twenty minutes east of downtown Los Angeles. Traveling north on Highway 5, go northeast on Route 605. If going south on Highway 5, exit at Route 60, go east, and exit at Crosswoods Parkway, go north on Workman (follow signs). Free parking and shuttle service are provided.

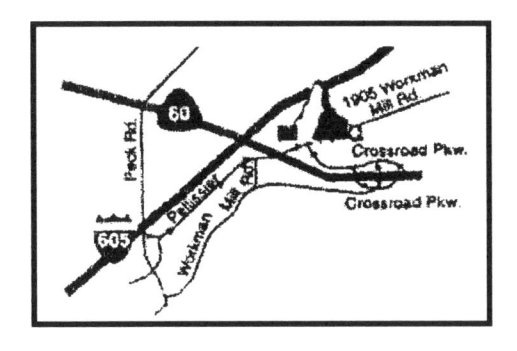

*For more information, contact:*
   Lilo Holzer
   United Swiss Societies of Southern California
   261 W. Kenneth Road
   Glendale, CA 91202
   Telephone: (818) 240-0970

*What to explore nearby:* Disneyland, Magic Mountain, Knott's Berry Farm, Getty Museum, San Diego Sea World, movie studios.

# Glenwood Springs, Colorado

## WEIHNACHTS FEIR
## CHRISTMAS PARTY

*Description:* This event is a European dinner with a European-style celebration of Santa Claus for children. In addition, a raffle is held, Christmas carols are sung, and Christmas dance music is played.

*Date of festival:* First Sunday in December

*Admission fee:* Price of your dinner

*Hours of festival:* 5:00 p.m. to 11:00 p.m.

*Year first conducted:* 1989

*Last year's attendance:* 70

*For more information, contact:*
    Rosemarie Bürki
    Vail/Eagle Valley Swiss Club
    P. O. Box 595
    Eagle, CO 81631
    Telephone: (303) 328-2374

## Vail, Colorado

## SWISS SKI CUP

*Description:* Cross-country skiers, apres skiers, and spectators are welcome at this annual ski outing. Trophies are given for top female and male skier. Usually given away are two Swiss watches and a pair of skis. Live music follows the awards ceremony.

*Location:* Nastar Ski Course at Hunky Dory

*Date of festival:* Last weekend in March before daylight savings time changes

*Admission fee:* About $7 for race; $4 for snack

*Hours of festival:* 8:00 a.m. to 5:00 p.m.

*Year first conducted:* 1989

*Last year's attendance:* 75 racers plus apres ski people

*For more information, contact:*
   Rosemarie Bürki
   Vail/Eagle Valley Swiss Club
   P.O. Box 595
   Eagle, CO 81631
   Telephone: (303) 328-2374

## 1st August Party

*Description:* Events include *steinstossen*, dinner, awards ceremony, alphorns, children's lampion parade, fireworks, dancing and singing, camping out, fishing, hiking, horseback riding, bratwurst, raclette.

*Location:* Sweetwater Lake Resort

*Date of festival:* The closest Saturday and Sunday to August 1 (most often before August 1)

*Admission fee:* About $10, members; guests, $15, guests

*Hours of festival:* 2:00 p.m. to ?

*Year first conducted:* 1989

*Last year's attendance:* 75

*For more information, contact:*
   Rosemarie Bürki
   Vail/Eagle Valley Swiss Club
   P. O. Box 595
   Eagle, CO 81631
   Telephone: (303) 328-2374

# Chicago, Illinois

## First Of August Celebration

*Description:* For this August first celebration, there will be games for children and also for adults. The menu will include bratwurst, *cervelat*, various salads, breads, and an original *Zuger Kirschtorte* for dessert, made by the Swissôtel. Domestic beer, soft drinks, and Swiss wines will be available. At dusk there will be a lampion parade for the children.

*Location:* American Legion Hall, 6140 W. Dempster, Morton Grove, Illinois

*Date of festival:* Saturday closest to August 1

*Admission fee:* About $20

*Hours of festival:* 4:00 p.m. to 9:00 p.m.

*Last year's attendance:* 200

*Directions:* Morton Grove is about a twenty-minute drive from downtown Chicago

*For more information, contact:*
Britta Renwick
Swiss Club of Chicago
P. O. Box 11921
Chicago, IL 60611-0921
Telephone: (773) 929-0864

## Swiss Week—Highlights of Switzerland

*Description:* At the time of publication, planning for this event was still underway. One theme of this event will be the celebration of the new sister city relationship with Lucerne. Tentative events will be a gala dinner, a Swiss village, and exhibit of Swiss products situated on Daley Plaza. Planned entertainment of the village may include wine and cheese tasting, a flag-throwing show (*fahnenschwingen*), arts and crafts, a milk "cow," a mobile bakery, a Wilhelm Tell presentation, alphorn blowers, yodelers from New Glarus, Wisconsin. In addition, there are plans to present several Swiss-related programs about visual arts, theatre, music, dance, film, and literature.

*Location:* Daley Plaza, downtown Chicago

*Date of festival:* September 9-19, 1999 (call below for information on subsequent years)

*Year first conducted:* 1999

*For more information, contact:*
Swiss Week, Ltd.
Consul General of Switzerland
737 North Michigan Avenue
P.O. Box 11561
Chicago, IL 60611-0561
Telephone: (312) 915-0061
Fax: (312) 915-0388

# Highland, Illinois

## SCHWEITZERFEST

*Description:* The festival is a midwestern U.S. town's untypical homecoming celebration with a distinct Swiss accent. The Swiss flag and Swiss cantonal flags decorate the central business area and also the homes of descendants of early Swiss immigrants. There is a parade each evening beginning at about 6:00 p.m. Following the parade there is a band concert. In addition to some Swiss activities, there are typical American carnival rides, other amusements, and American homecoming foods.

*Location:* Park Plaza, center of town

*Date of festival:* Second Saturday and Sunday in June

*Admission fee:* None

*Hours of festival:* Saturday, noon to midnight; Sunday, 2:00 p.m. to 10:00 p.m.

*Year first conducted:* 1968

*Last year's attendance:* 5000

*For more information, contact:*
Robert Bowman
Highland Junior Chamber of Commerce
25 Willow Creek Drive
Highland, IL 62249
Telephone: (618) 654-3245

## City of Highland
A Sesquicentennial City 1837-1987

## SWISS CHRISTMAS LIBRARY DINNER

*Description:* On the first Sunday evening in December, the Mercantile Bank of Highland sponsors a public Swiss dinner for the benefit of the Louis Latzer Memorial Library (1001 Ninth Street). The library is a memorial to the late founder of the Helvetia Milk Condensing Company, later known as the Pet Milk Company. The main floor of the library is converted into a Swiss banquet hall and is decorated with Swiss and Swiss cantonal flags and other Swiss decorations. The menu is typically American. Tickets are always sold out. The program is generally American music.

*Location:* Louis Latzer Memorial Public Library

*Date of festival:* First Sunday in December

*Admission fee:* $30

*Hours of festival:* 6:00 p.m. to 10:00 p.m.

*Year first conducted:* 1975

*Last year's attendance:* 200

*For more information, contact:*
　Terri Clayton, Chair
　c/o Mercantile Bank of Highland
　1000 Broadway
　Highland, IL 62249
　Telephone: (618) 654-8841; (618) 654-8859

# Berne, Indiana

## Swiss Days

*Description:* During this Swiss festival, the streets are dotted with merchants' displays; the aroma of Swiss specialty foods permeates the air; music and entertainment are performed on two stages; yodeling, *steinstossen*, horsepull, pedal tractor pull contests; bicycle rodeos; big wheel, foot races; basketball; tennis; golf tourneys; industry open house with tours; quilt, flower, garden, and art shows; South Adams High School auditorium musicals; parades; Swiss costumes; well-known polka bands with street dancing—everything adds up to fun-filled days for everyone.

*Location:* Downtown area

*Date of festival:* Last Friday and Saturday in July

*Admission fee:* None

*Hours of festival:* 9:00 a.m. to 11:00 p.m.

*Year first conducted:* 1972

*Last year's attendance:* 70,000

*Directions:* Berne is located about mid-state Indiana, slightly west of the Ohio line. Watch for horse-drawn vehicles when driving near Berne.

*About Berne:* On a beautiful but cold day, March 8, 1852, a company of Swiss Mennonites from the Bernese Jura district of Switzerland, where they were tenant farmers on the Münsterberg, gathered and bade farewell as the much talked-about trip to the new land, America, was about to take place. The desire to emigrate was attributable to several reasons. There had been a series of crop failures, rents were high, and perhaps most important, government had made strict military service laws to which these people, being peace-loving Mennonites, were strongly opposed.

On Friday, March 19, the group boarded the three-masted sailing vessel, the *Hahneman*, which carried no cargo except food, drinking water, wood, and coal, plus stones for ballast. There were 175 people on board. On the afternoon of April 29, they first saw land—America, the land of the free. April 30, after a doctor's examination, they were permitted ashore. The total fare from Basel, Switzerland, by way of Paris, to New York was $37.52.

Most of the persons in the group were members of the Sprünger family—brothers, sisters, cousins, brothers-in-law, and sisters-in-law. It was June and July when most of the twenty original families came to Indiana to settle in the area where Berne now stands.

The colony received a steady stream of Swiss immigrants each year, and as the population increased, many English-speaking people decided to settle here. Together, all made a contribution to a bigger and better community.

Today, Berne, Indiana, with a population of four thousand inhabitants, has realized a steady growth of business and industry, but at the same time has retained customs and characteristics from the immigrant forefathers from Switzerland, making it an exceptionally attractive city in which to live, work, play, and visit.

*For more information, contact:*
  Deb Horton
  Berne Chamber of Commerce

P. O. Box 85
Berne, IN 46711
Telephone: (219) 589-8080

*What to explore nearby:* While in Berne, visit its many Swiss theme shops and restaurants. Visit also the Swiss Heritage Village, a site north of town committed to the development of a living historical village which will cover life in the Berne community prior to 1902. Five buildings, including the oldest standing Mennonite church in Indiana, have been moved to the grounds and are being restored. In addition, a nature preserve and bird sanctuary have been developed at the site and scheduled nature walks through the woods are offered.

# Vevay (Switzerland County), Indiana

## SWISS WINE FESTIVAL

*Description:* Activities of the festival include grape stomping, *steintossen* (stone throwing), Edelweiss princess contest, parade, little Swiss polka dancers, wine tasting, children's pedal tractor pull. Throughout the festival professional Swiss entertainment is offered. Other events of this festival include a flea market, arts and crafts booths, horseshoe pitching contests, rides, concessions, 5K run, antique car display, rock and country music, and a fine beer and wine garden.

*Location:* Riverfront Park

*Date of festival:* Third or fourth weekend in August (Thursday evening through Sunday afternoon)

*Admission fee:* $1/person (entrance to grounds)

*Hours of festival:* Thursday, 6:00 p.m. to 11:00 p.m.; Friday, noon to 2:00 a.m.; Saturday, 8:00 a.m. to 2:00 a.m.; Sunday, noon to 5:00 p.m.

*Year first conducted:* 1969

*Last year's attendance:* 20,000

*Directions:* Vevay is located on the banks of the beautiful Ohio River, halfway between Cincinnati, Ohio, and Louisville, Kentucky, at the juncture of Routes 56 and 156.

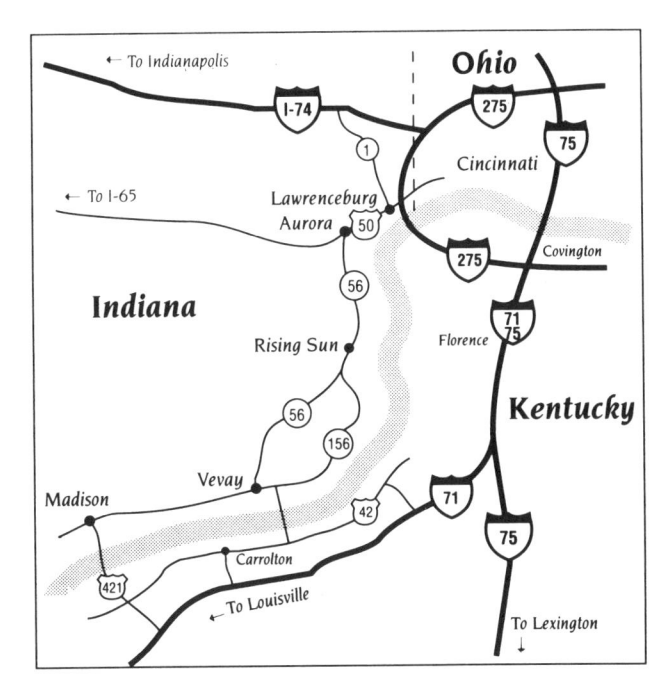

*About Vevay:* Vevay (pronounced Veevy) in Switzerland County, Indiana, is an Ohio River town of less than 2000 persons. Vevay traces its beginnings from a hardy group of seventeen Swiss-French settlers who migrated from the town of Vevey, Switzerland, on the north shore of Lake Geneva, in 1802. The Dufour, Golay, Berney, Meyland, and Boralley families formed an association to "cultivate the vine," long an art of the Swiss. They erected log cabins and began the cultivation of grapes. The grapes thrived in the rich sandy soil and the settlement grew as other immigrants came, establishing a small town which they named Vevay after their native city. Today, a portion of the downtown is listed on the National Register of Historic Places.

*For more information, contact:*
    Ann Mulligan, Welcome Center Director
    Swiss Wine Festival Committee
    P. O. Box 149
    Vevay, IN 47043
    Telephone: (812) 427-3237; (800) Hello VV
    Also: Kirk Works
    Telephone: (812) 427-3853

*What to explore nearby:* While in Vevay, visit the Switzerland County Historical Museum, the Hoosier Theatre, and historic homes and buildings on tree-lined streets overlooking the Ohio River. While hardly a place for night life, Vevay sports a remarkable range of architectural styles. The town has some 300 century-old buildings in a diversity of styles. Cream-colored signs throughout Vevay relate the history of its many structures. Visit the Ogle Haus Inn and enjoy the charm and warmth of a fine Swiss inn.

# Bethesda, Maryland

### HEIMATABIG

*Description:* The *Heimatabig* offers a memorable evening of Swiss traditions conducted by a talented and accomplished folklore group. It features a fine Swiss dinner and folklore performances of Swiss singing (in five languages), Swiss dancing, a display of over twenty different *trachten* (costumes), *fahneschwingen* (flag swinging), and *alphornblasen* (alphorn blowing). The Swiss Folklore Group of Washington, D.C., was formed to share the richness of Swiss culture and tradition with American audiences. Now listed in the National Folkdance Directory and the Washington, D.C., Folklore Society, this group is eager to stage performances throughout America.

*Location:* Parish Hall, Church of the Little Flower, 5607 Massachusetts Avenue, Methesda, Maryland

*Date of festival:* Second Saturday before Easter or Saturday after Easter

*Admission fee:* About $25

*Hours of festival:* 7:00 p.m. to midnight

*Year first conducted:* 1964

*Last year's attendance:* 350

*For more information, contact:*
Fran Walters
Swiss Folklore Group of Washington, D.C.
5704 Kingswood Road
Bethesda, MD 20814-1818
Telephone: (301) 530-5643

# Berne (West Concord), Minnesota

## BERNE SWISS FEST

*Description:* Swiss Fest typifies "The Charm of an Old World Festival" as it authentically celebrates the heritage of the Swiss settlers who came to the Berne, Minnesota, area over 100 years ago. Events for the family include the historical village, William Tell story, *fahnenschwingen* (flag throwing), *steintossen* (stone throwing), Swiss storytelling, alphorn blowing, *sackgumpen* (sack races), style show of Swiss costumes, stage performances and *schwingen* (Swiss wrestling). Demonstrations include alphorn blowing, *bauernmalerei* (Swiss painting), bobbin lace making, *scherenschnitte* (scissor cutting), bratzel making, flag throwing, and wood carving. Entertainment includes yodeling, Swiss dancing, alphorns, bell concerts, Swiss band, and a flag parade.

*Location:* Church grounds, Zwingli United Church of Christ

*Date of festival:* Saturday and Sunday, first weekend in August

*Admission fee:* $3 (adults), $1 (children 6-12), free (pre-school)

*Hours of festival:* Saturday, 11:00 a.m. to 9:00 p.m.; Sunday, 11:00 a.m. to 4:00 p.m.

*Year first conducted:* 1953

*Last year's attendance:* 2500

*About Berne:* Many Swiss traveled as Casper Solomon did; that is, directly from Europe's shore to New York and then inland. Solomon left Berne, Switzerland, and went to Le Havre, France. He sailed from Le Havre and arrived at New York forty-eight days later. Casper Solomon first stopped at a settlement in Ohio, then trekked west to Green County, Wisconsin. The Green County area (including the settlements of New Glarus and Monroe) was the first Swiss settlement in the region. From Green County, Solomon forged ahead to the Berne, Minnesota, area, considered the third Swiss settlement in the area. On January 6, 1872, about twenty families gathered in the old schoolhouse in Berne to hear a sermon by Rev. George Kurtzmann. Following the service, the Zwingli Evangelical and Reformed Congregation of Milton Township, Door County, Berne, Minnesota, was formed. In ten years, the membership increased to about fifty parishoners.

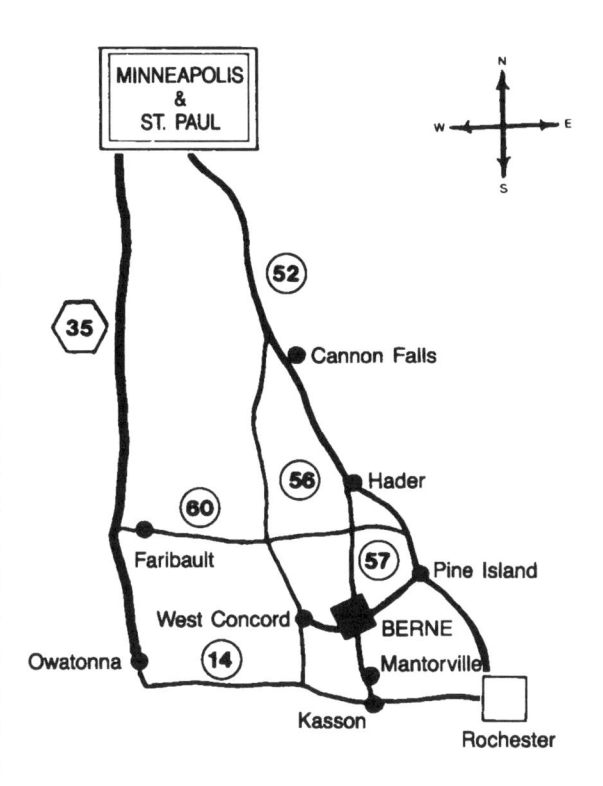

*For more information, contact:*
    Sam E. Ellson
    R.R. 1, Box 186
    Kasson, MN 55944
    Telephone: (507) 635-5563

*What to explore nearby:* Visit historic Mantorville and step back in time to see this village listed on the National Register of Historic Places. Mantorville is south of Berne on Highway 57. Also nearby in Rochester is the Mayo Clinic.

# Brooklyn Park, Minnesota

## NEW SCHWANDEN SWISS FAMILIES REUNION AND PICNIC

*Description:* This annual festival celebrates the early Swiss pioneers who settled the area of New Schwanden, Hennepin County, Minnesota, in 1854. The park exhibits Swiss decorations and flags. Dinner is potluck. Other events are Swiss music with yodeling and an alphorn player, a large family tree chart, histories, and pictures. There are games and prizes for all, young and old alike.

*Location:* Oak Park Grove

*Date of festival:* Third Saturday in August

*Admission fee:* $3 per family

*Hours of festival:* 10:00 a.m. to 8:00 p.m.

*Year first conducted:* 1978

*Last year's attendance:* 55

*Directions:* Go west from the Mississippi River on I-694 to Brooklyn Boulevard. Then take Zane Avenue north through Brooklyn Center to Brooklyn Park. Oak Grove Park is at the intersection of 6941 Zane Avenue, North and 102nd Avenue, North. At the park entrance will be a Swiss flag. From Champlin, Minnesota, go east on Route 12 for 2.25 miles, then north on Route 14 on Brynes Drive, which changes to Zane Avenue, north. Proceed for two miles to park entrance.

*About New Schwanden:* The would-be New Schwanden emigrants left Schwanden, Canton Glarus, in August 1853 and spent fifty days at sea before arriving in America. They traveled to the Swiss town of New Glarus, Wisconsin, to look for land, but found that most of it was already claimed or too costly. With little money left, they worked their way toward Minneapolis (then known as St. Anthony Falls) and arrived in April 1854. In June 1854, they found the land they claimed and began cutting logs to build their cabins. On March 25, 1855, they moved into their cabins and called the vast area New Schwanden. These early settlers were John Blesi, Peter Blesi, Martin Hosli, Hilarious Schmid(t), John U. Tschudi, and Fridolin Zopfi.

*For more information, contact:*
   Wayne C. Blesi, President
   New Schwanden Swiss Families Association
   3109 Boone Avenue, North
   New Hope, MN 55427-2420
   Telephone: (612) 544-8535

# Rockford, Minnesota

## First Of August Picnic

*Location:* The Trechsel Residence, 7455 S. Lake Sarah Drive

*Date of festival:* Saturday nearest August 1

*Hours of festival:* 4:00 p.m. until mosquito time

*About Rockford Minnetonka:* This Swiss club was started by families who migrated from their homeland, some of whom have lived in Minnesota for twenty-five years. The Twin Cities Swiss American Association was founded on June 13, 1973. Currently there are about 100 family members who actively participate in several dinner meetings and this featured yearly picnic gathering. The club is growing and welcomes the participation and membership of any Swiss American related people in the Twin Cities area.

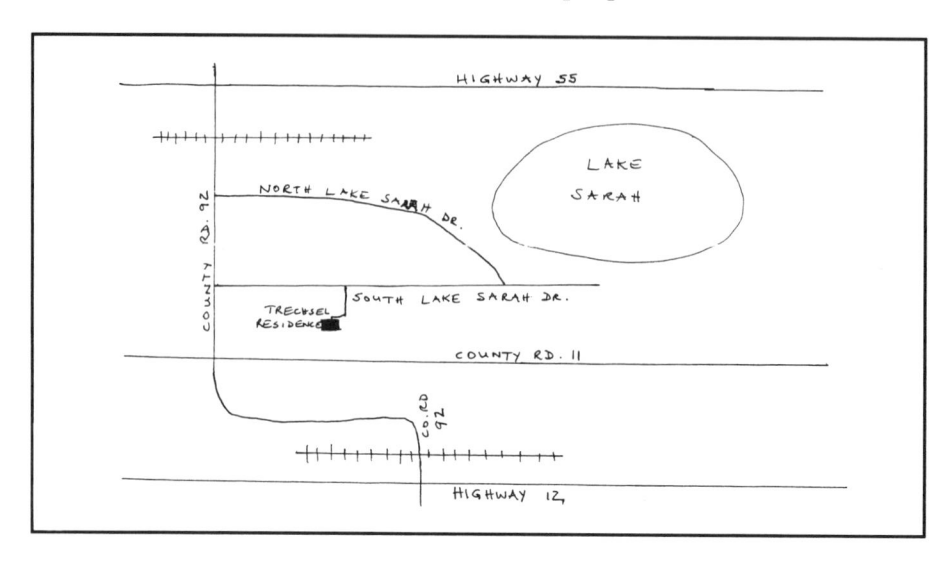

*For more information, contact:*
   Lony Maeder
   Twin Cities Swiss American Association
   2455 Brynes Road
   Minnetonka, MN 55305
   Telephone: (612) 546-2660

## Clarksburg, New Jersey

### FIRST OF AUGUST CELEBRATION

*Description:* This event includes reading of the message of the president of the Swiss Confederation, sing-along of familiar Swiss melodies, full-course dinner, dancing, and a lampion parade for children (bring your own lampion).

*Location:* Clarksburg Inn

*Date of festival:* Date closest to August 1, but not Friday, Saturday, or Sunday

*Admission fee:* None (pay for dinner)

*Hours of festival:* 5:30 p.m. to 9:00 p.m.

*Year first conducted:* 1981

*Last year's attendance:* 130

*For more information, contact:*
　Ida M. Graf Urbank
　Swiss Club of the Jersey Shore
　18 Downing Street
　Toms River, NJ 08755
　Telephone: (908) 349-5792

# New York, New York

## KAFFEEKLATSCH FOR SWISS SENIORS

*Description:* The traditional *Kaffeeklatsch* is a social gathering around coffee and tea for sharing and discussion. All Swiss seniors and their friends are cordially invited.

*Location:* Swiss Inn

*Date of festival:* Third Wednesday of each month (except June, August, and December). On these three months other events take place at a different time.

*Admission fee:* None. Please call a few days in advance to confirm date, location, and your attendance.

*Hours of festival:* 2:00 p.m. to 4:00 p.m.

*Year first conducted:* 1983

*Directions:* The Swiss Inn is located at 311 West 48th Street, near 8th Avenue, New York City. Parking is available next door.

*For more information, contact:*
  Swiss Benevolent Society
  608 Fifth Avenue, Room 309
  New York, NY 10020
  Telephone: (212) 246-0655

## ANNUAL SWISS BANQUET AND BALL

*Description:* This is a formal "black tie" banquet and ball honoring a different canton each year. Program includes a welcome by the President of the Swiss Society of New York and greetings by members of the ambassadorial and Consul General staff and other dignitaries. Following dinner is dancing and Swiss music. During the evening there is a drawing of an extensive group of excellent raffle prizes.

*Date of festival:* Last Saturday in January

*Admission fee:* $185 (in 1999)

*Hours of festival:* 7:00 p.m. to midnight

*Last year's attendance:* 300

*About New York:* In October 1882, a number of Swiss immigrants joined together to found the New York Swiss Club. These Swiss immigrants were attracted by the opportunity for family and friends to get to know each other and build new contacts and membership in the New York area as well as in Switzerland. Within a very few years, the club became the center of the Swiss Colony of New York. Long-time residents met to exchange ideas, newcomers were welcomed, young people were guided, and the elderly were assisted. On May 30, 1930, the Swiss Club and the Swiss Scientific Society merged and created the Swiss Society of New York. From the beginning the Society has fostered friendships among its members and between the United States and Switzerland. One important event toward this goal is the annual Swiss Banquet and Ball. Wherever you might reside, you are invited to consider membership in the Swiss Society of New York.

*For more information, contact:*
   Annemarie Gardin, President
   Swiss Society of New York
   633 Third Avenue, 30th Floor
   New York, NY 10017-6706
   Telephone: (212) 944-5951; (212) 840-0974

## SWISS JASS CHAMPIONSHIP "SWISS CUP"

*Description:* Jass is the national Swiss card game enjoyed by all ages. This championship tournament is the largest and oldest in the United States. In this *schieber* tournament partners are assigned by random numbers and are changed after every hand. The Swiss Cup (*Wanderpreis*) will be awarded to the tournament winner and the Coupe Bovay (*Wanderpreis*) plus cash will be awarded for the highest hand.

*Location:* (see contact person)

*Date of festival:* Second weekend in April

*Admission fee:* $20 (including lunch). Advance reservations are absolutely necessary.

*Hours of festival:* 10:00 a.m. to 5:00 p.m.

*Year first conducted:* 1977

*Last year's attendance:* 50

*For more information, contact:*
    Annemarie Gilman
    Swiss Benevolent Society of New York
    608 Fifth Avenue, Room 309
    New York, NY 10020
    Telephone: (212) 246-0655

## SWISS BENEFIT DINNER

*Description:* The Annual Benefit Dinner is a gala fundraising event in support of the Swiss Institute's programming. The Swiss Institute is a non-profit cultural center, founded in 1986 to foster artistic dialogue between Switzerland and the United States. The Swiss Institute hosts six exhibitions per year, a series of jazz and classical concerts, lectures, readings, film and video screenings, dance performances, and other cultural events. The Benefit Dinner is an important source of support for the programs.

*Date of festival:* May of each year in New York, N.Y. (exact location varies)

*Admission fee:* Dinner, program, dessert, dancing, and wine, under $100. Tickets are limited and reservations are required.

*Hours of festival:* From 6:00 p.m. onwards

*Year first conducted:* 1989

*Last year's attendance:* 200

*Directions:* Location varies; sometimes in Swiss Institute Gallery

*For more information, contact:*
    Christine Crowther, Administrative Manager
    Swiss Institute
    495 Broadway
    New York, NY 10012
    Telephone: (212) 925-2035

*What to explore nearby:* Guggenheim Museum SoHo, Chinatown, and SoHo Galleries are all within walking distance.

## SWISS NATIONAL DAY CELEBRATION

*Description:* Attractions include Swiss musical entertainment and a children's playground with supervised activities. A Swiss Marketplace will offer crafts and consumer goods. Bratwurst, *cervelats*, and other Swiss specialty foods will be available. Raffle tickets will be sold for many fine prizes, including Swiss Air flights to Switzerland, watches, etc. Program will include welcoming addresses by members of the ambassadorial staff and a traditional lampion parade.

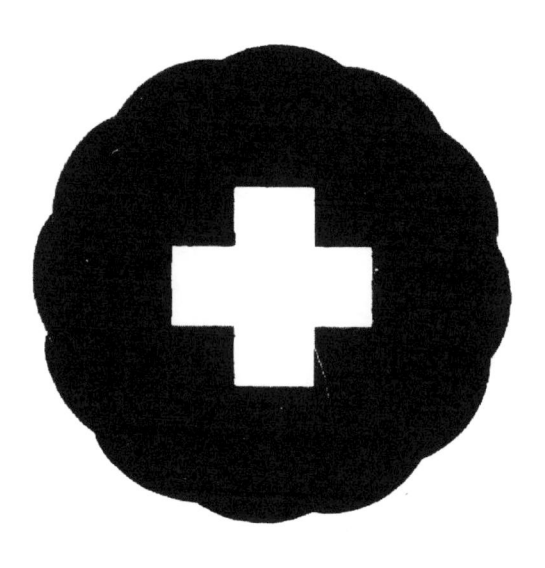

*Location:* Germania Park, Dover, New Jersey

*Date of festival:* August 1, if this falls on a Saturday, or last Saturday in July preceeding August 1

*Admission fee:* $4 per person over age 12

*Hours of festival:* 1:00 p.m. to 7:00 p.m.

*Year first conducted:* Many years ago

*Last year's attendance:* 1500

*Directions:* Using public transportation, take New Jersey transit trains from Penn Station to Dover, or take the Lakeland bus from the Port Authority to Dover. A free shuttle bus will operate between the Dover terminals and Germania Park.

*About New York:* The Swiss Benevolent Society began in 1830, and until 1873 was closely allied with the Swiss Consulate of New York. The purpose of the Society was to serve two main functions: one social, the other philanthropic. Until the mid-1850s, the Society could cope with the demands on its financial resources, but by the end of the 1850s an economic slump resulted in severe unemployment, all the while that immigration remained high. Soon after Spring 1883, the Society acquired a home of its own. Relief seekers were fed and lodged at this home. Thanks to excellent relations with railroad and steamship companies, the Society was able to provide low-cost transportation to immigrants who needed to travel west, or to those who wanted to return to Switzerland. The home soon became a permanent home for old Swiss who were poor, alone, or unable to fend for themselves.

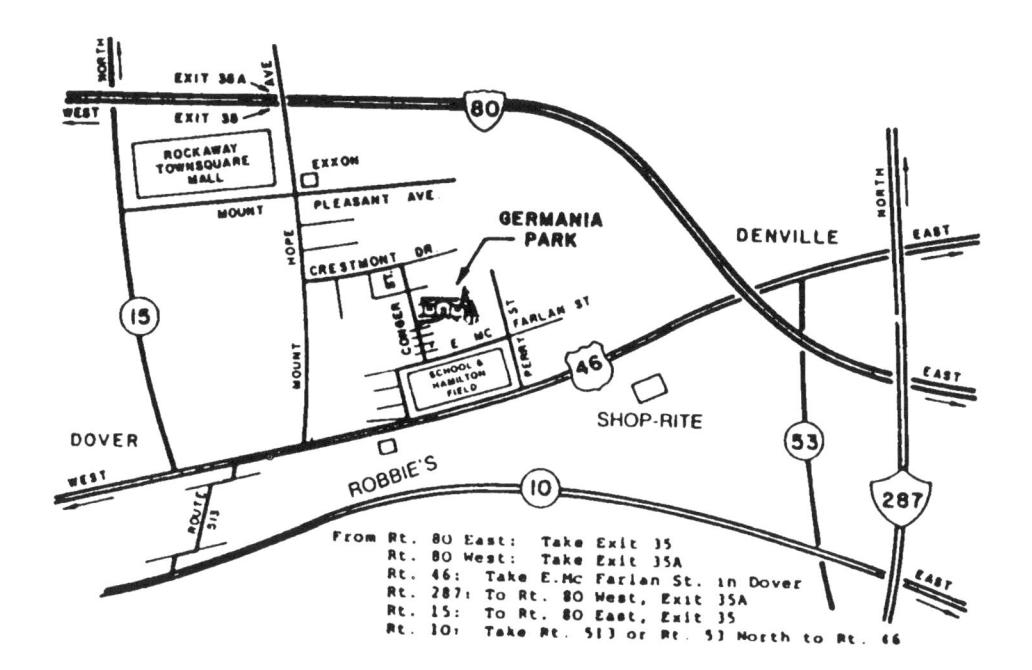

*For more information, contact:*
   Annemarie Gilman
   Swiss Benevolent Society of New York and Swiss Ski Club
   608 Fifth Avenue, Room 309
   New York, NY 10020
   Telephone: (212) 246-0655

# Columbus, Ohio

## ANNUAL SWISS CLUBS DINNER AND CONCERT

*Description:* Every year the Alpenrösli Society and the Grütli Verein sponsor an event for all the Swiss Clubs in central Ohio and other persons interested in Swiss culture. The founding Swiss organization in Columbus is the Grütli Verein in 1870. The Alpenrösli Society was founded in 1890. A short business meeting is held by the sponsoring organizations, and this is followed by a well-known speaker on Swiss history, culture, or genealogy. Recent speakers were Delbert Gratz, retired professor at Bluffton College (Ohio), and Erdmann Schmocker,

**In Unity There Is Strength**

president of the Swiss-American Historical Society. The speaker's program is followed by two Swiss choirs performing in Swiss costume. The evening concludes with a multi-course meal of Swiss and American foods.

*Location:* (see contact below)

*Date of festival:* First Sunday in December

*Admission fee:* About $15 per person

*Hours of festival:* 4:00 p.m. to 9:00 p.m.

*Year first conducted:* 1931

*Last year's attendance:* 200

*About Columbus:* The Columbus Grütli Verein for men, founded in 1870, is the forerunner of all the five Swiss societies in the Columbus area and is one of the oldest Swiss organizations in the state of Ohio. The Swiss Ladies Aid Aldenrösli Society was founded in 1890. The founding purpose of these organizations is to "bring its members more closely in harmony and friendship by mutual support in cases of financial need, sickness, and death, and to foster culture and sociability." The activities of these societies consist of monthly meetings, programs, fund-raisers, and projects to foster fellowship, the appreciation of Swiss heritage, the portrayal of Swiss culture in central Ohio, research into Swiss genealogy and family history, and to provide for general needs of the Swiss Clubhouse.

*For more information, contact:*
    Annemarie Wenger
    Swiss Home Association
    351 East Gates Street
    Columbus, OH 43206
    Telephone: (614) 443-3607

# Sugarcreek, Ohio

## OHIO SWISS FESTIVAL

*Description:* This festival features continuous free entertainment on two stages by Swiss musical groups, yodelers, and polka bands. Festival visitors can enjoy a fine parade and such typical Swiss sports as *steinstossen* (stone-throwing) and *schwingen* (wrestling). In addition, there is a large craft show and free dancing in the pavilion. There will be a yodeling contest and costume contests with prizes awarded for the largest group in Swiss costume, the oldest, the youngest, and the person who has traveled the greatest distance. Swiss cheese is sold in sandwiches or by the pound. Meals are served in the huge cafeteria and feature barbequed chicken and bratwurst dinners. Don't miss the tasty apple fritters sold at the First Mennonite Church tent. With thirteen Swiss cheese factories located in the area, Sugarcreek is recognized as the leader of the Swiss cheese industry in Ohio and a leader in Swiss cheese production in the United States. To give recognition to this, a Swiss cheese exhibit is prepared, a Swiss Cheese Chase (five-mile run) is conducted, and a Grand Champion Cheesemaker is named.

*Location:* Downtown streets of Sugarcreek

*Date of festival:* Each year, fourth Friday and Saturday after Labor Day

*Admission fee:* $4 per car; $20 per bus

*Hours of festival:* Friday, noon to 11:00 p.m.; Saturday, 10:00 a.m. to 10:00 p.m.

*Year first conducted:* 1953

*Last year's attendance:* 10,000

*Directions:* Sugarcreek (the "Little Switzerland of Ohio") is located on Ohio Route 39 in the rolling hills of western Tuscarawas County, Ohio, six miles west of Dover off I-77, and eighteen miles east of Millersburg.

*About Sugarcreek:* The Amish people first settled this area and started dairy farming. The German-Swiss were looking for a place to settle and chose Sugarcreek because of its similarity to home. These settlers were cheesemakers and could make good use of the milk produced by the Amish. Sugarcreek buildings have Swiss design and the local stores sell various Swiss and Amish wares. Sugarcreek has the largest brickmaking industry east of the Mississippi.

*For more information, contact:*
    Patricia Kaser, Information Coordinator
    Ohio Swiss Festival, Inc.
    P. O. Box 158
    Sugarcreek, OH 44681
    Telephone: (330) 852-4113

*What to explore nearby:* The entire area surrounding Sugarcreek is rich in Amish, Swiss, and Separatist culture. Nearby is an early Indian settlement. Consider visiting nearby Holmes County, home of the largest Amish community in the United States.

# Toledo, Ohio

## Swiss Picnic

*Description:* This is a magnificent annual picnic that features barbequed chicken, bratwurst, knockwurst, cakes and pastries, live German/Swiss music, and face painting for children. The Toledo United Swiss Societies, founded in 1869, is one of the oldest Swiss organizations in America.

*Location:* Oak Shade Grove, Oregon, Ohio

*Date of festival:* Sunday of first weekend in June

*Admission fee:* None

*Hours of festival:* Noon to 8:00 p.m.

*Last year's attendance:* 500

*For more information, contact:*
    Richard "Red" Hardt
    Toledo United Swiss Societies
    3663 Lynbrook Drive
    Toledo, OH 43614
    Telephone: (419) 385-5007

# Mt. Angel, Oregon

## OKTOBERFEST

*Description:* This festival, the oldest and longest-running Oktoberfest in Oregon and the largest folk festival in the northwest, celebrates Mt. Angel's Swiss and Bavarian heritage. The festival begins with a traditional German *Webentanz* (Maypole dance) performed daily by Mt. Angel school children. The streets of downtown Mt. Angel are lined with over sixty food chalets, each with rich, delicious Swiss and Bavarian treats: succulent sausages, sandwiches, pretzels, homemade pies, and other pastries and desserts. A select group of artists proudly display their handcrafted works for your purchase. There is interactive entertainment for the whole family in the Alpine Microgarten with lots of Swiss-style bands in the family Weingarten and the adults-only 18,000-square-foot Biergarten. A free Kindergarten on Saturday and Sunday will delight children of all ages with rides, clowns, magic shows, puppeteers, and a 4-H petting zoo. Free Swiss and Bavarian entertainment abound on the village bandstand, featuring all the great sounds of the Alpine country. Each day free concerts in German, Latin, and English are given at St. Mary's Gothic Church. Sports fans can enjoy softball, golf, volleyball, and a free 10K volkswalk sanctioned by the American Volkssport Association.

*Location:* The downtown streets of Mt. Angel, several buildings, city parks, the Parish Church, schools, gymnasiums, and the high school sports platz

*Date of festival:* From the second Thursday after Labor Day and ending on Sunday

*Admission fee:* None to festival; a small cover charge to the Biergarten, Weingarten, and Microgarten

*Hours of festival:* Thursday through Saturday, 11:00 a.m. to midnight; Sunday, 10:00 a.m. to 8:00 p.m.

*Year first conducted:* 1966

*Last year's attendance:* 350,000

*Directions:* From the north on I-5, take the Woodburn exit #271 and follow State Highway 214 to Mt. Angel (approximately ten miles). From the south on I-5, take the Market Street exit #256 at Salem and follow signs to State Highway 213. Proceed east through Silverton to Mt. Angel (approximately sixteen miles).

*About Mt. Angel:* Mt. Angel was first settled in 1867 by a group of German Catholic pioneers and then, soon after in 1881, by German Swiss Benedictines. The nearby Mt. Angel Abbey was founded by Benedictine monks from Engelberg, Switzerland, Canton Obwalden. Benedictine sisters from the convent of Maria Rickenback in Switzerland founded the Queen of Angels Monastery, a site on the National Registry of Historic Places. The Benedictine Abbey, monestery, library, and seminary are still the community's foundations.

*For more information, contact:*
  Jerry Lauzon, Director
  Oktoberfest
  P. O. Box 437
  Mt. Angel, OR 97362
  Telephone: (503) 845-6882

*What to explore nearby:* The city of Mt. Angel (population 2930) is centrally located in the lush Williamette Valley and is within forty-five minutes from downtown Portland and within ninety minutes of the Oregon coast and the ski slopes of the Cascade range. Salem, the state capital, is seventeen miles south of Mt. Angel. Also, fifteen miles south of Mt. Angel is Silver Falls State Park, a major national park with trails, camping, and magnificent falls.

# Portland, Oregon

## PORTLAND SCHWINGFEST

*Description:* On Saturday, the park opens at 9:00 a.m.; wrestling begins at 11:00 a.m. and continues until late afternoon, followed by a *steintossen* (stone throwing) contest. Dinner in the evening is followed by a dance and the crowning, in traditional Swiss style, of the *Schwingfest* winners. Sunday features a barbeque, a tug-o-war, a jass tournament, kids' games, jam session, bingo, and a drawing of the raffle prize.

*Location:* Paesano Cedarville Park, Gresham, Oregon

*Date of festival:* First Saturday and Sunday weekend in August

*Admission fee:* About $7 per person

*Hours of festival:* 9:00 a.m.

*Year first conducted:* 1918

*Last year's attendance:* 400

*About Portland and western Oregon:* The Swiss community in western Oregon can trace its roots all the way back to the pioneer days of the Pacific Northwest. A few Swiss had migrated north after the California gold rush of 1849, and as Portland became settled in the 1850s, immigrants began arriving in larger numbers. In 1857, a number of Swiss, mainly Mennonites from Bern, founded colonies at Cedar Mill, Bethany, and West Union in Washington County. Other Swiss communities such as Hillsdale, Phillips, and Helvetia also were soon established. These Swiss immigrants found the fertile valleys and forested hillsides similar in many ways to their homeland. During the last quarter of the nineteenth century, economic hard times in Europe and the promise of new opportunities in America brought several thousand Swiss immigrants to western Oregon and southwestern Washington. The abbey and college at Mount Angel ("Engelberg") were founded during this period by a group of Benedictine monks. The brothers of the order came from the historic original Swiss cantons of Uri, Schwyz, and Unterwalden. Their success in agriculture induced many farmers from these cantons to settle in the area. During the course of the twentieth century, Swiss immigrants have continued to settle in this area. The topography, climate, and fertility of the land have been found especially desirable by Swiss farmers, dairymen, and fruit growers, while the larger cities have provided industrial and technical opportunities for skilled Swiss workers. Swiss-Americans living in the Portland area, from the early pioneers to those of us today, have always been proud of the heritage we have retained from the "Old Country." The early immigrants quickly formed various clubs and organizations to preserve the traditions of their homeland. Some of these clubs were the forerunners of the current Portland Swiss, Inc. Now, as then, we strive to retain the spirit of Switzerland.

*For more information, contact:*
    Dave Emmenegger, President
    Portland Swiss, Inc.
    13617 S. W. 62nd Avenue
    Portland, OR 97219

# Spartanburg, South Carolina

## SWISS WEEK AND SWISSFEST

*Description:* An estimated 10,000 visitors attended Swiss Week '98, which included about 5,000 visitors at the Swissfest "August 1st Celebration." Featured were performances of the Swiss National Men's and Women's Olympic Gymnastics teams and the musical entertainment *(stimmung)* of the Calanda Band from Switzerland.

*Location:* Spartanburg, South Carolina

*Date of festival:* The week containing August 1

*Last year's attendance:* 10,000

*For more information, contact:*
Swiss-American Society of the Piedmont
P. O. Box 480
Spartanburg, SC 29304

# Gruetli-Laager, Tennessee

## ANNUAL SWISS REUNION AND CELEBRATION

*Description:* Activities of the day include slides of local mountains and parks, tours of the remaining Swiss farms and homes, a covered dish dinner, researching family history, fun, fellowship, and music. You may wish to bring pictures, artifacts, and family stories to share. Mountain wine and cheese will be available for tasting. For the covered dish dinner bring some of your favorite Swiss foods to sample and share. Plans are underway to develop a museum. This Swiss community was recently featured in an issue of the *Tennessee Magazine*.

*Location:* Swiss Memorial School

*Date of festival:* End of July

*Admission fee:* $10 (Society membership)

*Hours of festival:* 1:00 p.m. to 10:00 p.m.

*Year first conducted:* 1973

*Directions:* The Swiss Memorial School is located about twenty-two miles northeast of Monteagle, and Interstate 24, and approximately six miles east from junction 56 and 108, off Highway 108.

*About Gruetli-Laager:* In 1869, Peter Staub (1827-1904) was instrumental in the founding of Grütli in Grundy County, Tennessee. By 1886, this settlement counted 330 Swiss among its 400 inhabitants.

*For more information, contact:*
   Jacob Suter, Jackie Lawley, or Rose Stampfli
   Swiss Historical Society of Grundy County
   HCR 76, Box 142
   Gruetli-Laager, TN 37339
   Telephone: (931) 779-3295

# Midway (Heber Valley), Utah

## SWISS DAYS

*Description:* This festival of Swiss culture features music by the Swiss Choir Boys, dancing in traditional costume, lots of wine, Swiss foods, and other Swiss specialties. Each year a "Swiss Miss" is elected. Most of those performing music during Swiss Days are direct descendants of the early Swiss settlers in Midway.

*Location:* Midway Town Center

*Date of festival:* Labor Day weekend

*Hours of festival:* Each day, noon to 6:00 p.m.

*Directions:* The Heber Valley is located about fifty miles southeast of Salt Lake City. From Salt Lake City drive east on Interstate 80 for about twenty-five miles, then south on U.S. 40 about twenty miles to Heber City. Midway is about four miles west of Heber City on State Highway 113.

*About Midway:* Midway got its name when Mormon pioneers came to the valleys of Utah with a plan to develop a string of villages running from north to south. But Heber Valley, then known as Provo Valley, was left unsettled. Starting about 1858, settlers began raising cattle in areas to the north and south, namely Mound City and Cottonwood. However, problems with the Indians worried the church leaders in Salt Lake City and they advised the two communities to join together for safety, leaving out of the discussion which town should move. The solution was for them to relocate halfway, and that is how the new town got its name of Midway. Many of the farmers who settled this area in the early 1850s were from Switzerland. They developed their farms around the "hot pots" or warm springs of geothermal water which were thought to have curative powers, and which also were used for baptisms. Music has long played an important role in Midway. The early settlers did not all speak the same language, but they were able to communicate through music. The first brass band in Midway was organized by Andreas Burgener, a former bandmaster of the Swiss Military Band and a convert to the Mormon Church. One hundred years later this community band still exists. Here is a sampling of the Swiss family names of those who settled Midway in the nineteeth century: Abegglen, Aplanalp, Buehler, Burgi, Durschi, Harfeli, Hassler, Haueter, Huber, Kuhni, Murri, Naegeli, Siefert, Sulser, Wintseh, Zweifel.

*For more information, contact:*
   Britt Wild
   Swiss Days Celebration
   P. O. Box 279
   Midway, UT 84049

# Salt Lake City, Utah

## PACIFIC COAST SWISS SINGING AND YODELING FESTIVAL

*Description:* The Pacific Coast Singing and Yodeling Festival is a gathering of 1000 Swiss-American singers, yodelers, alphorn players, folk musicians, and their fans. Annually in a four-day event, they perform in a grand concert and participate in an all-day Swiss folk festival. The stated mission of the festival is fourfold: 1) to perpetuate the rich heritage of Swiss tradition; 2) to develop bonds of friendship among Swiss expatriates and participants; 3) to enrich the cultural fabric of America; 4) to raise funds to facilitate the growth and development of the host society (for 1999, the Edelweiss Swiss Chorus, Salt Lake City, Utah).

*Location:* At various locations in the western United States (in 1999, Salt Lake City, Utah, Festival Headquarters: Doubletree Hotel, 255 South West Temple)

*Date of festival:* June 17-20, 1999 (the Swiss Folk Festival will be on June 19 in Midway, city townhall, and nearby park)

*Admission fee:* $175-$200 for singing societies

*Hours of festival:* The 1999 festival begins on Thursday evening with a reception and banquet, and ends on Sunday with a closing ceremony and banquet.

*Year first conducted:* 1934

*Last year's attendance:* 5000

*Directions:* From Interstate I-15, exit 600 south and turn left on West Temple. Proceed to the Doubletree Hotel reception area.

*About Salt Lake City, Utah:* Salt Lake City was founded on July 24, 1847, by a group of Mormon pioneers (Mormons are members of The Church of Jesus Christ of Latter-Day Saints). The pioneers, led by Brigham Young, were the first non-Indians to settle permanently in the valley. They came to this valley in search of a region where they could practice their religion, free from hostile mobs and persecution. Many of the pioneers were European converts to Mormonism. During the decade of 1848-1858 these people brought their own culture, language, and skills to the valley, eventually building Salt Lake City into a cosmopolitan center.

*For more information, contact:*
    Ruth Schmazz Vorwaller, President
    1999 Pacific Coast Swiss Singing and Yodeling Festival
    1182 South Foothill Drive, #535
    Salt Lake City, UT 84108
    Telephone: (801) 583-7091

*What to explore nearby:* Historic Temple Square, Museum of Church History and Art, Family History Library, Beehive House, Cathedral of the Madeleine, the Great Salt Lake, University of Utah, State Capitol, Fort Douglas.

# Tacoma, Washington

## FALL SCHWINGFEST

*Description:* The Fall Schwingfest is the main event of the year and brings together wrestlers and other Swiss factions from all over the Pacific West Coast and Switzerland. This function is held in August, and is a two-day event on a Saturday and Sunday; however, the park grounds are open during the prior week and can accommodate up to thirty-two trailer hook-ups for the duration of the activities. The hall will be open on Friday evening at 7:00 p.m. with tape music and bar refreshments until midnight. On Saturday the gate opens at 9:00 a.m. and wrestler registration begins at 10:00 a.m., followed by competition starting at 11:00 a.m. for juniors and seniors. The kitchen opens at 11:00 a.m. and will serve delicious food and refreshments throughout the day. The evening dance begins at 9:00 p.m. featuring a local Swiss orchestra. During the evening dance on Saturday at approximately 10:00 p.m., a presentation is made of the senior and junior wrestlers and a crown of laurel wreaths and acorns is presented to the top senior winners by a bevy of beautiful crown girls. Medals are presented to the top junior winners, also by individually selected crown girls. The kitchen closes at midnight and the bar closes at 1:30 a.m. On Sunday the gate opens at 8:30 a.m. for a morning breakfast served until 10:30 a.m., and followed by an outdoor Catholic mass at 11:30 a.m. Wrestler registration begins immediately following mass, with competition starting at 12:00 noon for boys. The kitchen opens at 12:30 p.m. and will serve delicious food and refreshments throughout the day. The boys are awarded medals and certificates immediately following the wrestling on Sunday afternoon, usually by 5:00 p.m. The evening dance begins at 8:00 p.m., featuring a local Swiss orchestra. The kitchen closes at midnight and the bar closes at 1:00 a.m. Other events that are typical during the Fall Schwingfest include alphorn playing, flag tossing, and stone throwing (*steinstossen*). These are contests that all started at about the same period of time as the wrestling by the cow herders in the high Alps of Switzerland.

*Location:* Bonney Lake

*Date of festival:* Saturday and Sunday, second weekend in August

*Admission fee:* Saturday, about $7 per person; Sunday, about $6 per person

*Hours of festival:* 9:00 a.m. until dancing ends at 2:00 a.m.

*Year first conducted:* 1929

*Last year's attendance:* 1500

*For more information, contact:*
    Tony Rufener
    Swiss Sportsmen's Club of Tacoma
    7711 Dean Street West
    Tacoma, WA 98467
    Telephone: (206) 472-9106

# Helvetia, West Virginia

## Fasnacht

*Description:* Fasnacht is an old Swiss ritual observed every year to chase away winter and welcome Spring. It is celebrated the Saturday before Ash Wednesday in February with a Swiss feast and foot-tapping Appalachian music. We all, Helvetians and visitors, don costumes for a masked ball. The scarier the costumes, the better, because the idea is to drive Old Man Winter away. You can bring your own costume or rummage around in an attic here to see what you can find.

*Location:* Helvetia Community Hall

*Date of festival:* Always the Saturday before Ash Wednesday (February)

*Admission fee:* $4

*Hours of festival:* 5:00 p.m. to 12:00 p.m.

*Year first conducted:* 1869

*Last year's attendance:* 350

*Directions:* To reach Helvetia by car: I-79 to Buckhannon (thirty-four miles to Helvetia). Rt. 20 to French Creek (State Game Farm), Rt. 46 to Helvetia. The route from French Creek is well marked. Don't take any short cuts! If you're coming by way of Elkins, W.Va.: Rt. 250S, turn right at

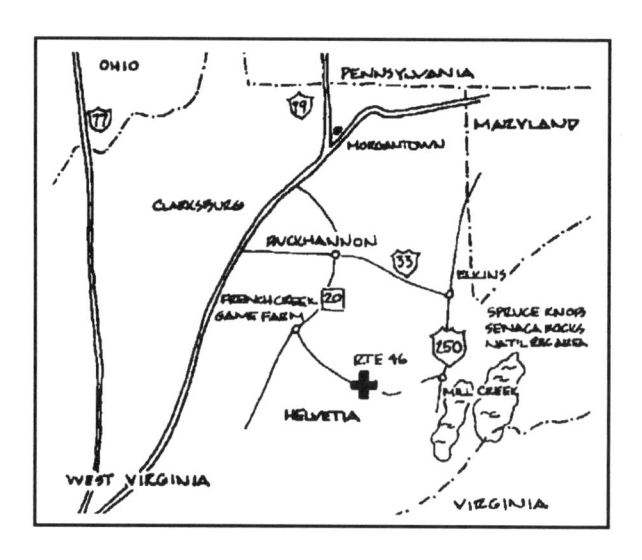

Millcreek, Rt. 46 to Helvetia; don't take any short cuts! If you fly into Elkins, we'll be happy to meet the plane.

*About Helvetia:* Following the Civil War, Mr. Isler, a member of the Brooklyn, N.Y., Grütli Verein, was a surveyor of thousands of acres in the mountains of West Virginia. Six members of his Verein decided to send a committee to investigate this distant area as a place of residence. These men were: Jacob Halder, Ulrich Mueller, Henry Asper, Sr., Joseph Zielman, Xavior Holtzweg, and Mathias Marti.

Leaving Brooklyn, N.Y., on October 15, 1869, the committee traveled by rail as far as Clarksburg, W. Va., the nearest railroad station to their destination. From there they traveled southward by wagon, horseback, and on foot, a distance of seventy-five miles, following the trail to the Hyer plantation. On October 20, 1869, they arrived at a lonely spot on the Middlefork River. Upon arrival, the outlook was very discouraging. There was nothing but wilderness all around them. The few local inhabitants, however, were very hospitable and encouraged the travelers to stay. Provided that the travelers would encourage immigration by others, land was offered at a reasonable price and offers were to help in settlement. All this was reported back to those still in Brooklyn, and, after due deliberation, all members decided to emigrate to West Virginia. The settlers who came from abroad had a fine education in the basic trades. Among the original settlers were persons with the following trades: Ulrich Mueller, Chris Zumbach, and Mathias Suesli, stone masons; Xavior Holzweg,

Christof Schilling, B. Merkli, Henry Eckart, and John Karlen, carpenters; John Toegler, blacksmith; Charles Fisher and J. V. Nachtigar, wagon makers; Fred Waelehli, botanist; Kasper Metzner, gardener; C. E. Lutz, architect; J. J. Mosman, designer; Henry Lehman, artistic painter; J. J. Hassig, painter; Gotlieb Daetwyler, shoemaker; Henry Asper, Sr., and Jacob Fobbes, tailors; Mathias Marti, hat maker; Herman Schloo and Joseph Zielman, watchmakers; George Betz, grocery salesman; John Andregg, baker; John Hoffer, confectionery baker; John Teuscher and Jacob Halder, cheese maker; Ernest Mathies, bookkeeper, G. O. Salinger, instrumental music and voice instructor; Christen Wenger and John Loser, German schoolteachers; Dr. Andrew Kern, minister; C. F. Stucky, doctor.

The year 1870 brought a few more settlers; however, at the beginning of 1871 there were only thirty-two persons in the community. In 1870 came the Andereggs and Kuerners. In 1871 came the Welchlies and Hofers from Ohio and the Teuschers, Blaties, Stutzmanns, Senhausers, Oschmans, along with C. E. Lutz from Pennsylvania. In the years 1873-1874, several families came directly from Switzerland. They were the Karlens, Gobelis, Torglers, Jacob Andereggs, Wuerzers, and others. As a result of active advertising of the new settlement by C. E. Lutz, people moved in from as far west as Iowa and as far north as Canada. From the west came the Fahrners, Dr. C. F. Stuckey, Wengers, Zumbachs, Vogels, Haslebachers, Burkeys, and Merklis. From Canada came the Daetwylers and Gimmels. Families arriving after the community was well established are the Betlers, Kunetzlers, Schluenigers, Süeslis, Fishers, Eckhards, Schneiders, and Steigers. At the close of 1874, there were ninety Swiss and German families residing at or near Helvetia for a total of 380 persons.

*For more information, contact:*
Eleanor Fahrner Mailloux
Helvetia Restoration and Development, Inc.
Box 42
Helvetia, WV 26224
Telephone: (304) 924-6435

**WE'RE GETTING READY FOR YOUR VISIT TO**

# Helvetia

## HELVETIA FAIR

*Description:* The Helvetia Fair is a real country event. The second weekend in September our local farm families set up farming displays with lots of flowers and fresh produce. We even have a parade with decorated farm wagons, homemade floats, and farm animals. It's a great way to meet some of our local characters and join in the fun, unless you'd rather just relax in the hammock at the Inn and listen to the Buckhann on River.

*Location:* Helvetia Community Hall

*Date of festival:* Always second weekend in September

*Admission fee:* $4

*Hours of festival:* Noon Saturday to 4:00 p.m. Sunday

*Year first conducted:* 1913

*Last year's attendance:* 550

*For more information, contact:*
    Eleanor Fahrner Mailloux
    Helvetia Fair Association
    Box 42
    Helvetia, WV 26224
    Telephone: (304) 924-6435

*What to explore nearby:* We are proud of our Swiss heritage and work hard at maintaining our traditions and customs. You might like to know that Helvetia was the first district in the state to be placed on the National Register of Historic Places. We have preserved ten historic buildings. One of them, an original settler's cabin, is now a museum filled with artifacts, including the original Swiss flag our ancestors brought when they settled here in 1869.

The Hutte Restaurant, heated by a wood stove, is filled with Swiss and American antiques, but the best part is the food. The Swiss are hearty eaters, and the fare at the Hutte is true to that tradition. We have a full menu, of course, but you'll want to try many of our homemade Swiss specialties. The Hutte is open every day from noon to 7:00 p.m., but our Sunday country brunch, called *Bernerplatte* is a real Swiss delight. You'll want to make reservations; we can only seat forty-eight, so call before you come.

The Beekeeper Inn isn't for everybody, but our guests seem to enjoy having breakfast served around the potbellied stove in the kitchen. Our three bedrooms with private baths are furnished with wonderful old antiques, but you won't find a phone or TV. We do have a checker game, cards, and some art supplies in the living room, and some books. The Inn, the former home of Helvetia's original beekeeper, is open seven days a week, all year. It's small (three bedrooms with private baths), but very cozy, so please call for reservations.

Augusta Heritage Center: Located on the campus of Davis and Elkins College (Elkins, W.Va.), the Augusta Heritage Center is devoted to presenting traditional music, crafts, dancing, and folklore.

All within easy driving distance are the following: Black Water Falls, Cannan Valley, Dolly Sods, Cranberry Glades, Cass Railroad, and Greenbanks. Also nearby is the Kum Brabo State Forest (ten miles), Holly River State Park (fifteen miles), and the state game farm (twenty miles).

# Alma, Wisconsin

## SWISS SUNDAY

*Description:* Potluck dinner is served at noon. Entertainment is flag throwing, alphorn playing, and music provided by a local family. Children can practice flag throwing and *Talerschwinge*. Stories are told of early Swiss migration to the area. In addition, there is a program on a topic related to Swiss history of the area.

*Location:* Harmonia Park (near Waumandee) on Highway E, eighteen miles southeast of Alma

*Date of festival:* Third Sunday in July

*Admission fee:* None (bring a covered dish to share)

*Hours of festival:* Noon to 5:00 p.m.

*Year first conducted:* 1992

*Last year's attendance:* 80

*Directions:* Alma is midway between LaCrosse and Eau Claire, Wisconsin, and is located on the Great River Road (Highway 35). To Harmonia Park, take Highway E southeast out of Alma and go about eighteen miles. Allow plenty of time as the roads are hilly and winding. Harmonia Park (near Waumandee) contains a large singing society hall surrounded by large pine trees.

*About Buffalo County:* By 1847, Buffalo County had one of the largest Swiss populations in the state. The census of 1890 showed that 680 Swiss lived in the county. The adjoining Mississippi River provided much needed transportation. After the founding of Alma and Fountain City, later immigrants moved to the bluffs and valleys which may have reminded them of their homeland. In addition to agriculture, jobs were available in the lumbering camps and rafting on the Chippewa and Mississippi Rivers.

*For more information, contact:*
    Blanche L. Schneider, Coordinator
    Swiss Residents of Buffalo County, Wisconsin
    1001 Second Street South
    Alma, WI 54610
    Telephone: (608) 685-4876

*What to explore nearby:* Merrick State Park at Fountain City on Highway 35; the town named "Tell" on Highway 37 between Alma and Mondovi; lock and dam #4 at Alma; Buena Vista Park at Alma on Highway E.

# Monroe, Wisconsin

## GREEN COUNTY CHEESE DAYS

*Description:* From the sound of the first alphorn to the echo of the last yodel, Cheese Days in Monroe will take you on a walk through time, where Old World charm and tradition meet with New World ideas. Since 1914 the "Swiss Cheese Capital of the U.S.A." has extended a warm *wellkommen* to an ethnic festival recognizing the cheese industry and honoring the Swiss ancestry, whose enterprising venture in cheesemaking in this country led to the area's world prominence in the cheese industry today. Visit the Historic Cheesemaking Center, where you can almost hear the clanging of the milk cans. Don't miss the Old World cheesemaking demonstration where a 200-pound wheel of Swiss cheese will be made outdoors in a copper kettle. Go from past to present as you wander into the lush, rolling countryside on the cheese factory and farm tours. See first-hand Green County's dairy and cheesemaking industries as they are today. The Monroe Swiss Singers Folk Fair will be held at the beautiful, historic Turner Hall, with its authentic Swiss architecture and examples of Swiss folk art and culture. Artisans will exhibit and demonstrate various Swiss folk art and traditions, including cabinetry and woodworking, woodcarving, *Bauernmalerei* (decorative Swiss folk painting), ethnic foods and pastries, *Scherenschnitte* (paper cutting), and more. Take a historic tour of Turner Hall and see the *Ratskellar* where cow bells hang over the bar, learn the history of the groups that make up Turner Hall and the area's heritage. Don't forget a visit to the *Wystube* where Old World ambiance lingers. The picturesque downtown square will come alive with accordion music, yodeling, alphorns, singing, dancing, and *Talerschwingen*. There will be an opening ceremony, arts and crafts, cow milking contest, 5K and 10K runs, cheese sales tent, vintage car display, golf classic, spectacular parades, food, street dances, and more. A fun-filled family weekend to delight the young as well as the young-at-heart.

The golf classic is open to the public and will be held Friday at the picturesque PGA-recognized Monroe Country Club. Tee times are between 11:00 a.m. to 3:00 p.m. The $75 fee includes eighteen holes of golf, cart rental, package of golf balls, and 1st Biennial Cheese Days embroidered golf shirt. Pre-registration guarantees shirt day of event.

Cheese Days opening ceremony is 5:00 p.m., Friday, and will feature alphorns, parade of flags, the official welcome by Mayor Bill Ross, and a memorial dedication.

*Location:* Downtown Monroe's Historic Square

*Date of festival:* Third weekend of September (even numbered years)

*Admission fee:* There is no gate fee. Other fees: golf classic, $75; Cheese Factory and Farm Tours (10 and older), $2; Cheese Days Balls, $5; 5K and 10K runs, $15; Swiss Folk Fair (10 and older), $1.

*Hours of festival:* Friday (noon to 1:00 a.m.), Saturday (9:00 a.m. to 1:00 a.m.), Sunday (9:00 a.m. to 6:30 p.m.)

*Year first conducted:* 1914

*Last year's attendance:* 200,000

*Directions:* Monroe is situated forty-two miles south of Madison, Wisc. (take Highway 151 to Route 69 to Monroe). From Chicago, take Northwest Tollway (I-90) almost to Rockford, Ill. Exit at U.S. 20 to Freeport, Ill. Then take U.S. 26 to Wisconsin state line where U.S. 26 becomes Route 69, which takes you into Monroe. The festival is located in downtown Monroe's Historic Square area. If coming from Madison, from Highway 69 turn left on 11th Street. If coming from Chicago, from Highway 69 turn right on 11th Street. Continue ten blocks on 11th Street and this will bring you to the downtown area.

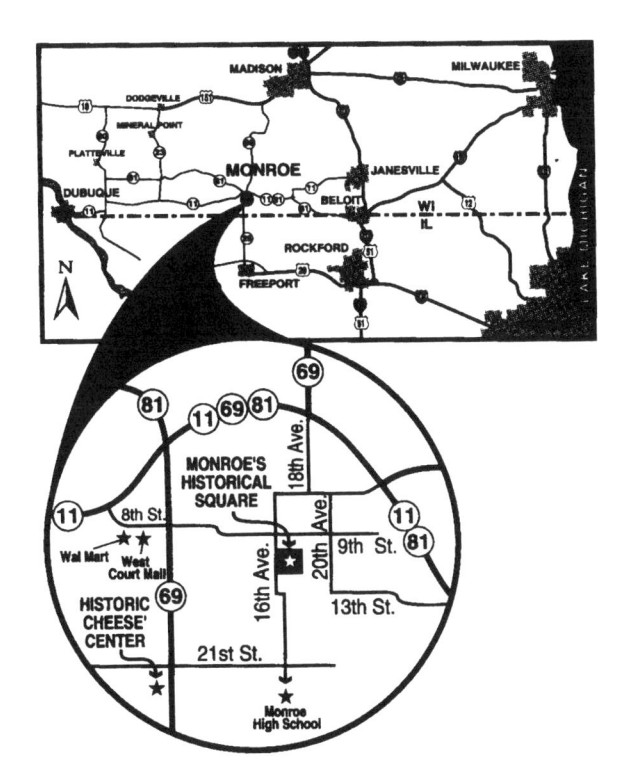

*About Monroe:* In 1845, 108 Swiss settlers came to the Green County area. Their main occupation was cash farming until about the time of the Civil War, when an invasion of insects cut the ground from under their main cash crop of wheat. Recognizing the lush, rolling, green hillsides as ideal for raising dairy cattle, each family purchased one cow for the price of $12 from their countrymen who had settled in Ohio. Soon they were not only making their own supply of cheese, but the first factory opened in 1869. Seven years later, in 1876, the area's cheesemakers were producing 225,000 pounds of Swiss and 775,000 pounds of Limburger per year.

Unfortunately, due to the offensive odor of Limburger, Monroe passed a law that made it illegal to move Limburger in or out of the city, or to store it here. This law almost drove one of the soon-to-be largest industries right out of town!

In 1873, Arabut Ludlow, a local businessman and banker, invited all the area's cheesemakers to his home, which is known today as the Ludlow Mansion. Ludlow, a brass band, and the cheesemakers, with their wagon full of Limburger, paraded down to and around the courthouse square. Ludlow made a speech in which he announced loud and clear that cheese had come to Monroe to stay.

Also in the 1870s, a group of Swiss visitors came from Switzerland and were so impressed with the quality of the area's Swiss cheese, they designated Monroe as the "Swiss Cheese Capital of the U.S.A." In 1914, several businessmen visiting Sauerkraut Day in Forreston, Illinois, developed the idea of a similar event in Monroe, with cheese taking the spotlight.

The first official Cheese Days was held after only nineteen days of preparation. Termed a success, an estimated 3,000 to 4,000 enthusiastic people attended in spite of a cold and rainy day. Four varieties of cheese were made in the area and each of the four corners of the square were designated as a place where one of the four varieties of cheese sandwiches would be handed out. Seven hundred pounds of cheese and 200 pounds of coffee were served free to the crowd. Entertainment for the event included a band concert with the Monroe and Orangeville bands playing, Swiss wrestling, and a street dance.

The next Cheese Days, in 1915, had longer preparation time and an extensive program, which included four exhibition teams of Swiss wrestling, speeches by the governor of Wisconsin, Emmanual Philipps, Maidson's Mayor Kayser, State Dairy and Food Commissioner George Weigle, Parade of Society Circus, including Monroe businessmen, seven bands of music, circus features, and business floats. There was a Swiss warble by Alpine Quartet, Swiss turning, football game between Monroe and Darlington, balloon ascension, free dancing on the "world's largest dance floor," a demonstration of the "food value of cheese and attractive table dishes," and a dance at Turner Hall.

From the sound of the first alphorn, to the echo of the last yodel, Cheese Days is an ethnic festival recognizing the dairy and cheese industries and honoring the Swiss ancestry, whose enterprising venture in cheesemaking in this country led to what has become the area's world prominence in the cheese industry today.

So it will be, the continuation of music, entertainment, tradition, and *Gemutlichkeit* to keep alive within the hearts of each visitor a part of the heritage that has been so influential to this truly blessed community.

*For more information, contact:*
  Jan Benkert, Coordinator
  Green County Cheese Days, Inc.
  1116 17th Avenue, P. O. Box 606
  Monroe, WI 53566
  Telephone: (800) 307-7208

## SWISS FEST

*Description:* The Monroe Swiss Singers were organized in 1963 with nineteen charter members, eighteen of whom were Swiss or German immigrants. Of the nearly fifty current members from south-central Wisconsin and north-central Illinois, nine are still original members and almost all others are of Swiss descent. Deborah Krauss Smith, a second-generation Swiss descendant, has directed the group since 1985. Annually, the Monroe Swiss Singers showcase the finest of Green County's authentic Swiss music and entertainment, including new performers and longtime audience favorites. For 1998, following a procession of large Swiss cowbells, the fifty-four-voice Monroe Swiss Singers, directed by Deborah Krauss Smith, will open the program with several Swiss folk songs for mixed choir. Perennial favorites such as accordionists/yodelers Betty Vetterli and Martha Bernet with pianist Helen Krattiger will share the stage with newer performers Kaye Gmur and Nancy Troxler, duo-yodelers from New Glarus, and with Monroe instrumentalists Bill and Sally Lanz and John Wegmueller, who will play the *schwyzeroergeli*, a small Swiss button accordion. No Swiss Fest would be complete without the alphorn trio of John Colstad, Heinz Mattmann, and Mike Moser, and junior alphornists Andy and Nick Lanz. Also featured will be the four-part men's music of the *Maennerchor* New Glarus and the Swiss *jodels*, folk songs, musical coin-rolling, and shenanigans of the New Glarus Yodel Club.

The Monroe Swiss Singers are very pleased to have on the program the newly-formed *Kinderchor*, a New Glarus-based children's choir directed by Kaye Gmur and accompanied on the accordion by Nancy Troxler. The little charmers, ranging in age from two to eleven, have been learning traditional Swiss folk songs and have performed in several area events.

A "two thumbs up" rating for audience appeal goes to returning performers *das Gummischuhe* Orchestra, a German-style band comprised of Monroe High School instrumental students and directed by Randy Schneeberger. A special grand finale performed by all the singers and instrumentalists will feature an arrangement of "*Schweizerpsalm*," the Swiss national anthem, written especially for our Swiss Fest by local teacher, performer, and arranger Randy Schneeberger.

Following the program, all are invited for more *gemütlichkeit* with old-time dance music provided by the Steve Meisner Band.

*Location:* Turner Hall, 1217 17th Avenue; telephone: (608) 325-3461

*Date of festival:* First Sunday in November

*Admission fee:* About $7; $1 for students K-12

*Hours of festival:* 3:00 p.m. to about 9:00 p.m.

*Year first conducted:* 1966

*Last year's attendance:* 500

*Directions:* Turner Hall is located two blocks south of the downtown Historical Square

*For more information, contact:*
    Deborah Krauss Smith, Director
    Monroe Swiss Singers
    N 4512 Cold Springs Road
    Monroe, WI 53566
    Telephone: (608) 328-4838

## DEUTSCHER WEIHNACHTSGOTTESDIENST (GERMAN CHRISTMAS COMMUNION SERVICE)

*Description:* The congregation of St. John's United Church of Christ, assisted by the Monroe Swiss Singers, offers the beautiful *Deutscher Weihnachtsgottesdienst* each year, early in December. Featured in a 1997 issue of the *Wisconsin State Journal* (Madison), this service is conducted entirely in German and is rooted in the early traditions and heritage of St. John's Church, which was founded in 1862 by Swiss and German immigrants. Services were conducted in German until the 1920s, with the Christmas Day communion service in German continuing until 1955. The current German service was reinstituted in 1972 and has grown in attendance.

An English translation of the service is provided for those who do not speak German. In addition to the congregational singing of German-origin carols, the Monroe Swiss Singers will sing an arrangement of the lovely Austrian carol *"Still, Still, Still"* and the beautiful *"O Jesulein Suess, O Jesulein Mild"* by German composer J. S. Bach. There also will be a piece played by alphorns and organ. The ambiance of the beautiful sanctuary, the music, the sound of the language as Luke's version of the Christmas story is read, and the inspiring message will all add up to a one-of-a-kind experience for the soul, something that often gets lost in our modern-day observance of Christmas. Following the service is a time of fellowship with refreshments.

*Location:* St. John's United Church of Christ, 1724 14th Street, Monroe; telephone (608) 325-2165

*Date of festival:* First Sunday in December

*Admission fee:* A free-will offering is taken

*Hours of festival:* 2:00 p.m. to 3:00 p.m.

*Year first conducted:* Yearly since 1985 and five times previously

*Last year's attendance:* 200

*For more information, contact:*
St. John's United Church of Christ
1724 14th Street
Monroe, WI 53566
Telephone: (608) 325-2165

## CHRISTKINDLMARKT

*Description:* This traditional pre-Christmas bazaar is an occasion to do some fine shopping. Available will be better quality merchandise from around the world and from upscale area merchants. You will feel the spirit of Christmas and be treated to some goodies. Proceeds from this bazaar help in funding Turner Hall.

*Location:* Turner Hall, 1217 17th Avenue

*Date of festival:* A two-day event in early December

*Admission fee:* None

*Hours of festival:* 10:00 a.m. to 5:00 p.m. each day

*Year first conducted:* 1998

*Directions:* Turner Hall is located two blocks south of the Historical Square

*For more information, contact:*
 Marianna Fischer, Coordinator
 Telephone: (608) 527-5656

*What to explore nearby:* Monroe has a picturesque Romanesque-style courthouse which is in the center of the downtown shopping area. A few of the nearby stores are adorned with an alpine architectural motif. When in Monroe you definitely must visit Turner Hall. The original Turner Hall was built as an opera house. After a major fire in 1936, it was rebuilt in typical Emmental architecture. Recently it has undergone extensive remodeling and is the home of the Swiss-American Gymnasts, the Swiss Club, the Monroe Swiss Singers, and foreign-type cheesemakers. Try the *kasekuchen* (cheese pie) for which the Turner Hall is famous, along with a glass of beer brewed by a local brewery. The historic Cheesemaking Center is located in Monroe and adjoins the Recreation Trail. Visit Alp and Dell where you can buy "Green County Gold" (cheese) and see how this is made. The Swiss Colony, originators of fine food gifts by mail since 1926, is located in Monroe. New Glarus is located eighteen miles to the north.

# New Glarus, Wisconsin

## POLKAFEST

*Description:* Come to New Glarus as the residents roll out their dance floor for an annual Swiss Polkafest in the Village Park. Each year Polkafest organizers go to great lengths to bring together the best polka bands they can find for this dance-filled weekend. Usually featured is New Glarus's Roger Bright Band. Recently the Roger Bright Band was voted the number one polka band by the Wisconsin Polka Hall of Fame, as well as receiving this organization's Senior Achievement Award. Bright entertains for locals and visitors every weekend at the New Glarus Hotel. Often polka bands from Switzerland provide the dance music and perform evenings at the New Glarus Hotel. Throughout the weekend, you'll find lots of good music, food, and beverages.

*Location:* New Glarus Village Park

*Date of festival:* Third or fourth weekend in May

*Admission fee:* About $8 per day

*Hours of festival:* Saturday, early afternoon until 1:00 a.m.; Sunday, early afternoon until 10:00 p.m.

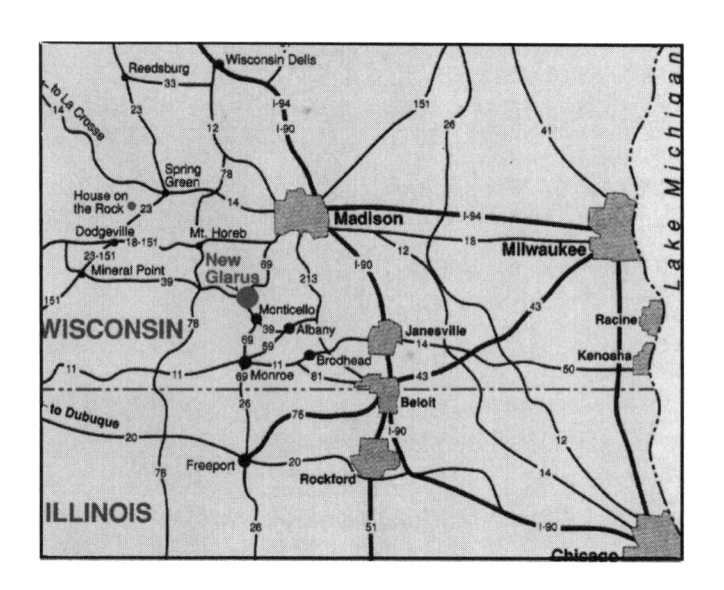

*Year first conducted:* 1988

*Last year's attendance:* 700

*Directions:* New Glarus, America's "Little Switzerland," is located in the rolling hills of Green County, Wisconsin, twenty-eight miles south of Madison, sixteen miles north of Monroe, on Highways 69/39. The drive from the Chicago area is about three hours, from Dubuque, two hours, from Madison, thirty minutes, and from Monroe, twenty minutes. From Chicago, take the NW tollway (I-90) to Beloit, Wisconsin. Exit I-90 onto I-43. Take I-43 west to the intersection of Highway 81. Follow Highway 81 west to the intersection of Highway 11. Follow 11/81 west to Monroe. Take the Monroe bypass to the New Glarus/Highway 69 north exit. Follow Highway 69 north to New Glarus. Free parking is available at the Tell festival grounds and a shuttle service is provided from New Glarus.

*For more information, contact:*
    Polkafest
    Box 713
    New Glarus, WI 53574-0713
    Telephone: (800) 527-6838 or (608) 527-2095

## HEIDI FESTIVAL AND LITTLE SWITZERLAND FESTIVAL

*Description:* In the Heidi Festival, all of the charm, humor, warmth, excitement, and drama of Johanna Spyri's great classic are performed by New Glarus's children, business people, housewives, and farmers in an unforgettable adventure rantging from the Alps to a palatial home in Frankfurt. See the heartwarming story of Heidi and her gruff grandfather, and watch their lives unfold in the majestic Swiss Alps. Live goats and kittens on stage are sure to delight young and old alike. A performance is given on each of three days.

Enjoy Old World traditions, such as alphorn playing, yodeling, folk dancing, and flag throwing at the Little Switzerland Festival Saturday evening. You've never heard anything like the haunting sound of alphorns. On Saturday and Sunday, pick your pleasure. The Craft and Art Fair will feature more than 100 vendors offering unique hand-crafted jewelry, clothing, wood carvings, and more. Find your treasures in the Flea Market on Saturday and Sunday at the Village Park.

Music and food will be in abundance all weekend. Sample local cheese, beer, bratwurst, European breads and pastries. On Saturday night, the streets of downtown New Glarus will close for the annual Street Dance. It's free, lively, and fun for the whole family.

*Location:* High School auditorium

*Date of festival:* Last full weekend in June

*Admission fee:* $6 each for general admission to the Heidi play and Little Switzerland Festival

*Hours of festival:* Heidi play: Friday, 7:30 p.m.; Saturday, 10:00 a.m. and 1:30 p.m.; Sunday, 1:30 p.m.; Little Switzerland Festival: Saturday, 7:00 p.m.

*Year first conducted:* 1964

*Last year's attendance:* 1500

*For more information, contact:*
    Heidi Festival
    P. O. Box 861, Dept. N
    New Glarus, WI 53574
    Telephone: (800) 527-6838

## VOLKSFEST
## (SWISS INDEPENDENCE DAY)

*Description:* Each year, New Glarus pays tribute to the birth of the Swiss nation on August 1, 1291. New Glarus actively maintains cultural ties to Switzerland by observing the Old World customs and traditions brought by the first settlers in 1845.

The Volkfest program includes Swiss singing, yodeling, flag throwing, *talerschwingen*, and accordion music performed by visiting groups from Switzerland, and by local residents dressed in authentic Swiss costumes. Dignitaries from Swiss consulates and the embassy in the United States, as well as officials in the Swiss government, have been featured speakers in New Glarus's Swiss Independence Day celebrations. Swiss music and entertainment follow the Volksfest presentations. Everyone is invited to join the dancing that continues throughout the day.

*Location:* Tell Shooting Park, one-half mile north of New Glarus on County Highway "0"

*Date of festival:* First Sunday in August

*Admission fee:* Adults, $5; children, $1; tickets are sold at the gate only

*Hours of festival:* Volksfest, 1:00 to 4:00 p.m.; dancing from 4:00 to 6:00 p.m.

*Year first conducted:* 1929

*Last year's attendance:* 1000

*For more information, contact:*
   Volksfest, New Glarus
   Visitor Information Center
   Telephone: (800) 527-6838 or (608) 527-2095

## WILHELM TELL PAGEANT AND ALPINE FESTIVAL

*Description:* The many Swiss festivals presented annually in New Glarus pay tribute to the Swiss customs and traditions preserved by the community since it was settled by Swiss immigrants in 1845. Community ties with Switzerland remain strong today, and the annual celebrations attract thousands of visitors—many from Switzerland—who enjoy the casual European atmosphere of this community. Labor Day weekend brings the Wilhelm Tell Festival. Schiller's play is presented three times in a beautiful outdoor amphitheater. The drama is presented by the people of New Glarus in the original German on Sunday and in an English version on Saturday and Monday. Presented for over sixty years, the colorfully-dressed cast of 200 (along with live goats, cattle, and horses) brings alive the story of how Wilhelm Tell, his arrow, and an apple helped Switzerland gain independence from the Hapsburg tyrant, Gessler. The pageant is preceded by entertainment provided by the Bell Ringers and the little Swiss Miss Dancers. The cast is comprised of local people, all of whom are amateurs, volunteering their time and talents. During intermission the Wilhelm Tell Usherettes (dressed in replicas of thirteenth-century cantonal costumes) perform folk dances.

On Saturday evening, enjoy traditional Swiss entertainment at the Alpine Festival in the new air-conditioned high school auditorium. Area residents in authentic costumes provide a unique program featuring alphorns, yodeling, and other Swiss music. On Sunday, there is an outdoor Art Fair in the Village Park, with activities for children and families. On Monday, a free ethnic fashion show is held, showcasing Swiss *trachten* (costumes) owned by local residents, along with costumes from the Tell Pageant. A village reminiscent of a small European town with beautifully designed Swiss architecture, New Glarus was recently chosen by the readers of *Wisconsin Trails* magazine as the "most picturesque small town in Wisconsin."

*Location:* Pageant: (Wilhelm Tell grounds, one mile east of Highway W, New Glarus); Festival: (New Glarus High School)

*Date of festival:* Saturday through Monday, every Labor Day weekend in September

*Admission fee:* For the Tell Pageant: $6 (reserved seat); $5 (adult general admission); $3.00 (children under twelve). For the Alpine Festival: $5, adults; $2 children; Saturday night camping: $15 per person

*Hours of festival:* Pageant: 1:00 p.m. (concludes by about 4:00 p.m.); Festival: 8:00 p.m.

*Year first conducted:* 1938

*Last year's attendance:* 3000

*Order reserved Tell drama and Alpine Festival tickets by contacting:*
  Peter Etter, President
  Wilhelm Tell Community Guild
  1420 Second Street, P. O. Box 456
  New Glarus, WI 53574
  Telephone: (608) 527-2810


## OCTOBERFEST

*Description:* Autumn is a special time in southern Wisconsin—fall colors, crisp air, apples and apple cider, pumpkins, a drive through the countryside. This Octoberfest is family oriented and interactive. Visitors are encouraged to participate in the hands-on activities such as cider pressing and other traditional fall season skills once necessary for life in rural Wisconsin. At the Village Park there are demonstrations of old-fashioned skills, and a program of Swiss music, yodeling, and alphorns. Weather permitting, you can try your luck at a round of bovine bingo.

The old town hall, one block north of the park, is transformed into a "General Store," hosting a bake sale, spinning, weaving, craft demonstrations, and local historical displays. Other weekend events include a harvest parade, hay rides, a barn dance with bluegrass/fiddle music, a hog roast/barbecue, brewery and winery tours, a Wisconsin author's book signing and sale.

*Location:* Village Park, New Glarus

*Date of festival:* Columbus Day weekend (second weekend in October)

*Admission fee:* None

*Hours of festival:* 10:00 a.m. to 5:00 p.m. (both Saturday and Sunday)

*For more information, contact:*
  New Glarus Visitor Information
  Telephone: (800) 527-6838
      (608) 527-2095

*About New Glarus:* In the 1840s, textile factories built in the lower valley replaced the cottage industry which had flourished in the upper regions of Canton Glarus, Switzerland. The crisis forced many Glarus residents to make a choice: become factory workers or settle on agricultural land in North America. On April 16, 1845, 193 people from all parts of Glarus set out on the long and dangerous journey to America. Travel arrangements were made through the Glarus Emigration Society, established with the aid of the Glarus government. Two scouts, Fridolin Streiff and Nicholas Duerst, were sent ahead to locate land suitable for the settlement for a colony of emigrants.

Impressed by the abundance of water, fertile soils, timber resources, and endless prairie, the scouts purchased 1200 acres of land in the Little Sugar River Valley in northern Green County and made preparations for the arrival of the immigrant settlers. On August 15, 1845, 108 members of the original party arrived in New Glarus. On their journey they had covered over 5000 miles.

Most immigrants were artisans and farmers, yet had to adapt to agricultural methods suited to the American farmland. Extreme climatic conditions and seasonal temperature variations had to be accommodated. By the 1880s, the establishment of a successful cheesemaking industry assured the community's survival. Other immigrants continued to join the original settlers and New Glarus prospered; the population today has grown to 1900. Today, the surrounding countryside is used primarily for dairy farming, and twenty-three cheese factories are scattered throughout Green County.

*What to explore nearby:* New Glarus offers amenities usually found only in larger communities. Motels, hotels, and bed and breakfasts are available in the village for overnight lodging. Tent camping ("go to sleep in New Glarus—wake up in Switzerland") is available on Saturday night on the Tell Festival grounds. Set up after 5:00 p.m., check out by 10:00 a.m. Sunday. Camping fee of $15/person includes a midnight snack, continental breakfast, and a Tell souvenir bread board made of native oak. Reservations are recommended. There are more than six restaurants offering Swiss cuisine, and many small shops offering a unique variety of imported European merchandise and locally-crafted items, as well as a large variety of locally made Swiss-style sausages, cheese, and Swiss pastries.

New Glarus supports two community museums and accommodates travelers enjoying the twenty-three mile Sugar River State Bike

Trail, headquartered in New Glarus. The Swiss Historical Village museum (a replica of a pioneer village) documents the Swiss emigration from Glarus, Switzerland, and the development of New Glarus after 1845. The twelve-building museum complex is packed with antiques and tools donated by families and businesses from the area. The Chalet of the Golden Fleece museum houses a unique private collection of items gathered from around the world by Edwin Barlow, one of New Glarus's more colorful residents and founder of the Wilhelm Tell play.

Swiss-style lodging is available in the New Glarus Hotel, the Chalet Landhaus, and several nearby bed-and-breakfasts. New Glarus is also well-situated as a staging point for regional exploration. It is close to the House on the Rock, Dodgeville, Spring Green, Mt. Horeb, Monroe, and Madison. It is on the way to Wisconsin Dells and several casinos.

# ENGLISH LANGUAGE BIBLIOGRAPHY

## A. SWISS FOLK TRADITIONS

Amstad, Werner. *Folk Traditions in the Swiss Mountains: Boys and Girls Depict Customs Practiced in their Villages.* Zürich, Switzerland: Union Bank of Switzerland, 1989.

(Video, 40 minutes) *Autumn Wine: A Fascinating Look at the Wines and Wine Festivals of Switzerland.* North Palm Beach, Florida: World Travel Video, 1981.

Chonz, Selina. *A Bell for Ursli.* New York, New York: H. Z. Walck, 1963. (A Swiss boy succeeds in finding a large bell to ring in the spring festival.)

*Christmas in Switzerland.* Chicago, Illinois: World Book, Inc., 1995.

Kramer, Paul. *Popular Customs and Traditions in Switzerland.* Zürich, Switzerland: Pro Helvetia, 1986.

(Video, 62 minutes) Lang, René. *Swiss National Customs.* 1995 order VHS-NTSC from Airborne AG, P. O. Box 116, CH-6212 St. Erhard, Switzerland.

Maur, Franz auf der. *Folklore in Switzerland.* Aarau, Switzerland: AT Verlag, 1988.

Schwabe, Erich. *Traditions and Popular Festivals in Switzerland.* Zürich, Switzerland: Swiss National Tourist Office, 1971 (reprinted here).

## B. Swiss Immigration And Swiss Settlements In North America

Abbott, John C. *Journey to New Switzerland: Travel Account of the Koepfli & Suppiger Family to St. Louis on the Mississippi & the Founding of New Switzerland in the State of Illinois.* By Joseph Suppiger, Salomon Koepfli, and Kaspar Koepfli. Translated by Raymond J. Spahn, with excerpts from Jennie Latzer Kaeser's translation of Solomon Köpfli, *Die Geschichte der Ansiedlung von Highland* (The Story of the Settling of Highland). Foreword by Joseph Blake Koepfli. Edwardsville, Illinois: Southern Illinois University Press, 1986.

Allen, James D. "Iowa's Little Switzerland," pp. 378-384 in *Annals of Iowa*, 30, July.

Allen County Public Library. *The Vevay Reveille-Enterprise.* Fort Wayne, Indiana: Allen County Public Library, 1986.

Anderhold, Joseph J. *The History of the Imperial Valley Swiss.* Holtville, California: Imperial Valley Swiss Club, 1984.

Anderson, Phyl & Schiesser, Mrs. Frank. *The History of the New Glarus Historical Society.* New Glarus, Wisconsin, 1976.

Agassiz, George R. (ed.). *Letters and Recollections of Alexander Agassiz, with A Sketch of His Life & Work.* Boston, Massachusetts: Houghton Miflin, 1913.

Alderfer, E. G. *The Ephrata Commune: An Early American Counterculture.* Pittsburgh, Pennsylvania: University of Pittsburgh Press, 1985.

Beam, C. Richard (ed. & transl.). *The Niklaus Joss Letters.* Second edition. Winesburg, Ohio: Nineteen Quinquenennial Winesburg Reunion, 1985.

Bettis, Norman C. *The Swiss Community of Highland, Illinois: A Study in Historical Geography*, Masters Thesis. Western Illinois University, 1968.

Billigmeier, Robert H. and Picard, Fred A. (eds.). *The Old and the New: The Journals of Two Swiss Families (Johannes Schwizer & Jakob Rütlinger) in the 1820s*. Minneapolis, Minnesota: University of Minnesota Press, 1965.

Bookholt, John H. *The Story of Mauch Chunk (Pa.), "The Switzerland of America," 1818-1918*. Thesis (M.A.), Lehigh University, 1951.

Bory, Jean-Rene. *Swiss in American Life*. Zürich, Switzerland: Foundation Pro Helvetia, 1977.

Bowen, Ralph H. (ed. and transl.). *A Frontier Family in Minnesota: Letters of Theodore & Sophie Bost, 1851-1920*. Minneapolis, Minnesota: University of Minnesota Press, 1981.

Carter, Dorothy E. "The Story of the Swiss Settlement in Dallas," *Texas Historical Teachers Bulletin*, Vol. XIII, (1925), pp. 77-80.

(Video) *Celebration of a Lifetime: New Glarus' 150th Anniversary*, That's Klassy, 1995, New Glarus Public Library, 319 Second Street, New Glarus, WI 53574.

Cornetti, Elisabeth. "Swiss Immigration to West Virginia, 1864-1884: A Case Study," *The Mississippi Valley Historical Review*, XLVII (June 1960), pp. 66-87.

Cordle, Charles G. (ed.). "The John Tobler Manuscripts: An Account of German-Swiss Emigrants in South Carolina, 1737," *Journal of Southern History*, Vol. V (1939), pp. 83-97.

Courten, Régis de and Rokicka, Wanda (eds.). *Switzerland and the United States of America*. Relations of Switzerland with the United States—Swiss Emigration. Bern: Schweizerische Landesbibliothek, 1964.

Daughters of the American Revolution, John Paul Chapter. *Revolutionary Soldiers of Switzerland County, Indiana*. Madison, Indiana: 1958.

Duerrenberger, Susanne. *Human Geographic Study of Swiss Immigrants in California*. Thesis (M.A.), University of Basel/California State University, 1994.

Dufour, Perret. *The Swiss Settlement of Switzerland County, Indiana.* Indiana Historical Collections, Vol. 13. Indianapolis, Indiana: Indiana Historical Commission, 1925.

Duls, Louisa D. *The Story of Little Switzerland (N.C.).* Richmond, Virginia: Whittet & Sheppardson, 1982.

Eshleman, H. Frank. *Swiss and German Settlers of Southeastern Pennsylvania.* 1991 reprint. Baltimore, Maryland: Genealogical Publishing Co.

Faust, Albert B. (ed.). "Documents in Swiss Archives Relating to Emigration to American Colonies in the Eighteenth Century," *American Historical Review*, Vol. XXII (October 1916), pp. 98-132.

Faust, Albert B. (ed.). *List of Swiss Emigrants in the Eighteenth Century to the American Colonies.* Vol. I: Zürich: 1734-1744. Washington, D.C.: The National Genealogical Society, 1920.

Faust, Albert B. "Swiss Emigration to the American Colonies in the Eighteenth Century," *American Historical Review*, 22 (October 1916): 21-41.

Faust, Albert B., and Braumbaugh, Gaius (eds.). *List of Swiss Emigrants in the Eighteenth Century to the American Colonies.* Vol. II: Bern: 1706-1795; Basel: 1734-1794. Washington, D.C.: The National Genealogical Society, 1925.

Fankhauser, N. G. *An Illustrated History of the City of Berne.* Berne, Indiana, 1926. (Thirtieth anniversary souvenir edition of the *Adams County Witness*, Vol. XXX (Sept. 3, 1926), No. 105.

Gratz, Delbert L. *Bernese Anabaptists and Their American Descendants.* Scottdale, Pennsylvania: Herald Press, 1953 (Reprinted 1994 by Masthof Press, Morgantown, Pennsylvania.)

Gustafson, Auburn M. (ed.). *John Spring's Arizona.* Tucson, Arizona: University of Arizona Press, 1966.

Hale, Frederick. *The Swiss in Wisconsin*, 1994 reprint. Madison, Wisconsin: State Historical Society of Wisconsin.

Hall, J. *Italian-Swiss Settlement in Plumas County 1860-1920*. Association for Northern California Records and Research, No. 1. Chico, California: California State University, Chico and Brock's Printers, 1975.

Haller, Charles R. *Across the Atlantic and Beyond: The Migration of German and Swiss Immigrants to America*. Bowie, Maryland: Heritage Books, 1993.

Hamilton, E. C. *The Story of Monroe* (Wisconsin), 1976. The Print Shop, Monroe Public Schools, Green County Welcome Center, 2108 Seventh Avenue, Monroe, WI 53566.

(Video, 60 minutes) *Helvetia: The Swiss of West Virginia*. The Augusta Heritage Center of Davis & Elkins College, Elkins, WV 26211, 1993.

Hewitt, John N. B. (ed.). *Journal of Rudolph Friedrich Kurz*. Smithsonian Institute, Bureau of American Ethnology, Bulletin 115. Washington, D.C.: Government Printing Office, 1937, Facsimile editions, Fairfield, Washington: Ye Galleon Press (1986?).

Hinke, William J. (ed. & transl.). "Report of the Journey of Francis Louis Michel from Bern, Switzerland, to Virginia, October 2, 1701-December, 1702." *Virginia Magazine of History and Biography* 24 (1916): 1-43; 113-141; 275-303.

Hofer, Genevieve, Mailloux, Eleanor, and Betler, Ella. *The Story of Helvetia Community, Randolph County, West Virginia*. Centennial History Committee, P. O. Box 15, Helvetia, WV 26226, 1969.

Jackson, Frances Helen. *The German Swiss Settlement at Gruetli, Tennessee*. Masters Thesis, Nashville, Tennessee, Vanderbilt University, 1933.

Jacobson, Gloria. *Two For America: The True Story of a Swiss Immigrant* (Children's Book), 1986. Roberts European Imports, 102 Fifth Avenue, New Glarus, WI 53574.

Jewett, Ruth H. *The Swiss Connection: The Lives & Times of Friedrick Joss & Emily Bigler Joss and Their Descendants*. Chicago, Illinois: Privately printed, 1983.

Kelsey, Rayner W. (ed.). *Cazenove Journal 1794: A Record of the Journal of Theophile Cazenove Through New Jersey and Pennsylvania* (transl. from the French). Haverford College Studies No. 13. Haverford, Pennsylvania: The Pennsylvania History Press, 1922.

Kioski, Bernard T. *The Recent Swiss Immigrants to Lincoln County, Wisconsin.* Thesis (M.A.), University of Wisconsin-Stevens Point, 1970.

Kleber, Albert. *History of St. Meinrad Archabbey, Foundation for the Monastery of Einsiedeln, 1854-1954.* American Benedictine Academy Historical Studies, Monasteries and Convents. St. Meinrad, Oregon: A Grail Publication, 1954.

Knittle, Walter A. *Early Eighteenth Century Palatine Emigration.* Philadelphia, Pennsylvania: Dorence & Co., 1937; reprint: Baltimore, Maryland: Genealogical Publishing Co., 1977.

Knox, Julie LeClerk. *The Dufour Saga 1796-1942: The Story of the Eight Dufours who Came From Switzerland and Founded Vevay, Switzerland County, Indiana.* Crawfordsville, Indiana: Howell-Goodwin Co., 1942.

Kollmorgen, Walter M. *The German-Swiss in Franklin County, Tennessee.* A Study of the Significance of Cultural Considerations in Farming Enterprises. (Dissertation, Columbia University, New York.) Washington, D.C.: Department of Agriculture, 1940.

Kuhni, Fred. *Immigration From Switzerland to Utah and His Life in Heber City and Midway, Utah.* Logan, Utah: Utah State University, 1974.

Kuhns, Levi Oscar. *The German and Swiss Settlements of Colonial Pennsylvania: A Study of the So-Called Pennsylvania Dutch.* New York, New York: Henry Holt, 1901.

Kummer, Marvin A. *The Swiss Colony Bernstadt.* Thesis (M.A.), University of Louisville, 1955.

Lehman, James O. *Sonnenberg, A Haven and a Heritage: A Sesquicentennial History of the Swiss Mennonite Community of Southwestern Wayne County, Ohio.* Kidron, Ohio: Kidron Community Council, 1969.

Leiding, Harriette D. K. "Purrysburg: A Swiss-French Settlement of South Carolina on the Savannah River," *Huguenot Society of South Carolina*, No. 39, pp. 27-39.

Lienhard, Heinrich. *From St. Louis to Sutters Fort, 1846*. (Translated and edited by Erwin G. and Elisabeth Gudde.) Norman, Oklahoma: University of Oklahoma Press, 1961.

Magee, Joan. *The Swiss in Ontario*. Windsor, Ontario: Electra Books, 1991.

Meier, Heinz K. *The United States and Switzerland in the Nineteenth Century*. The Hague: Mouton & Co., 1963.

Meier, Heinz K. (ed.) *Memoirs of a Swiss Officer (Rudolph Aschmann) in the American Civil War*. Transl. by Hedwig Rappolt. (Swiss-American Historical Publications, Vol. 4.) Bern, Switzerland: Herbert Lang, 1972.

Metraux, Guy S. *Social and Cultural Aspects of Swiss Immigration into the United States in the 19th Century*. Thesis (Ph.D.), Yale University, 1949.

Neff, Deborah, and Zarrilli, Phillip. *Wilhelm Tell in America's "Little Switzerland," New Glarus, Wisconsin*. New Glarus, Wisconsin: New Glarus Wilhelm Tell Community Guild, 48 pp., 1987.

Newbauer, S. C. "The Swiss Settlement in Madison County, Illinois." *Transactions of the Illinois State Historical Society*, 1906, pp. 232-237.

Pedrazzini, Clay. "The Italian Swiss of California," *The Swiss in the United States*, pp. 93-101. Madison, Wisconsin: Swiss-American Historical Society, 1940.

Pfaller, Benedict, "The Most Rev. Vincent Wehrle, D.S.B., D.D., First Bishop of Bismarck (1855-1941)," in Senn, Alfred (ed.) *The Swiss Record: Yearbook of the Swiss-American Historical Society*, Madison, Wisonsin: Swiss-American Historical Society, Volume II, March 1950, pp. 31-34.

*Presentation of a Flag, February 27, 1896, From the City of Bern, Switzerland, Founded in 1191, To the City of New Bern, N. C., U.S.A., Founded in 1710*. New Bern, North Carolina: N. S. Richardson, 1896.

Preysz, Clara M. "The Swiss Settlement at Alpena, West Virginia," *Randolph County Historical Society Magazine of History and Biography*, No. 9, 1937, pp. 33-37.

Ragatz, Lowell J. (ed. and transl.). "A Swiss Family in the New World: Letters of Jacob and Ulrich Bühler 1847-1877." *Wisconsin Magazine of History* 6 (1922-1923), pp. 317-333.

Ragatz, Lowell J. (ed. and transl.). "Memoirs of a Sauk Swiss, by the Rev. Oswald Ragatz." *Wisconsin Magazine of History* 19 (1935), pp. 182-227.

Rappolt, Hedwig (ed. and transl.). *An American Apprenticeship: The Letters of Emil Frey 1860-1865*. Afterword by Hans R. Guggisberg. New York, New York: Peter Lang, 1986.

Raup, H. F. "The Italian-Swiss in California, 1852-1950," *California Historical Society Quarterly*, 30 (1951), pp. 305-314.

(Video) Saurer, Karl. *Steinauer, Nebraska: Cycles of Gain and Loss*. Bank of Steinauer, P. O. Box 38, Steinauer, NE 68441.

Schelbert, Leo (ed.). *New Glarus 1845-1970: The Making of a Swiss-American Town (Travel Diary of Matthias Dürst)*. Transl. by Hedwig Rappolt. Glarus, Switzerland: Kommissionsverlag, Tschudi, AG, 1970.

Schelbert, Leo. *Swiss Migration to America: The Swiss Mennonites*. New York, New York: Arno Press, 1980.

Schelbert, Leo (ed.). *The United States and Switzerland: Aspects of an Enmeshment*. Yearbook of German-American Studies, Volume 25. Lawrence, Kansas: University of Kansas, 1991.

Schelbert, Leo. *America Experienced: Eighteenth and Nineteenth Century Accounts of Swiss Immigrants to the United States*. Camden, Maine: Picton Press, 1996.

Schenk, Paul. *The Colony Bernstadt in Laurel County, Kentucky, at the Beginning of Its Sixth Year*. Transl. by S. A. Mory, London: Kentucky, 1940.

Schiesser, Elda and Schiesser, Linda. *The Swiss Endure, 1845-1995* (New Glarus, Wisconsin). Roberts European Imports, 102 Fifth Avenue, New Glarus, WI 53572.

Schmocker, Erdmann. *Helvetia, Americana: U.S. Map Showing Swiss-Named Locations*. Private issue, 6440 N. Bosworth Avenue, Chicago, IL

Schoop, John C., "The New Helvetic Society Pennsylvania Chapter, 1938-1948," in Senn, Alfred (ed.) *The Swiss Record: Yearbook of the Swiss-American Historical Society*, Madison, Wisconsin: Swiss-American Historical Society, Volume I, March 1949, pp. 54-60.

Schoop, John C., "The Swiss Benevolent Society of Philadelphia," in Senn, Alfred (ed.) *The Swiss Record: Yearbook of the Swiss-American Historical Society*, Madison, Wisonsin: Swiss-American Historical Society, Volume II, March 1950, pp. 70-72.

Schulz-Behrend, George. "Andreas Dietsch and Helvetia, Missouri," in Senn, Alfred (ed.) *The Swiss Record: Yearbook of the Swiss-American Historical Society*, Madison, Wisconsin: Swiss-American Historical Society, Volume II, March 1950, pp. 5-30.

Schweizer, Max. *A Portrait of New Switzerland 1831-1900: Origin and Development of a Swiss Settlement in the United States of America (Madison, Illinois)*. Transl. by Harold & Lynne Schweizer. Zug, Switzerland: Zürcher Books, 1979.

Senn, Alfred, "Celebration in Madison, Wisconsin," in Senn, Alfred (ed.) *The Swiss Record: Yearbook of the Swiss-American Historical Society*, Madison, Wisconsin: Swiss-American Historical Society, Volume I, March 1949, pp. 61-70.

Smith, Henry A. M. "Purrysburgh." *The South Carolina Historical & Genealogical Magazine*, October 10, 1909: 187-219.

Spahn, Raymond J. (ed.). *The Swiss On The Looking Glass Prairie: A Century and a Half 1831-1981*. Compiled by Betty Spindler Coats. Foreword by Joseph Blake Koepfli. (Edwardsville, Illinois): Friends of the

Lovejoy Library, Southern Illinois University at Edwardsville and Highland Historical Society, 1983.

Spahn, Raymond, Spahn, Jürgen & Betty Alderton (eds.). *New Switzerland in Illinois as Described by Two Early Swiss Settlers Kasper Koepfli & Johann Jacob Eggen in Spiegel von Amerika und Aufzeichnungen aus Highland's Gründungszeit.* Foreword by John C. Abbott, Edwardsville, Illinois, Friends of the Lovejoy Library, Southern Illinois University at Edwardsville, Illinois, 1977.

Sprunger, Eva F. "Berne, Indiana," in Senn, Alfred (ed.) *The Swiss Record: Yearbook of the Swiss-American Historical Society*, Madison, Wisconsin: Swiss-American Historical Society, Volume I, March 1949, pp. 25-26.

Sprunger, Eva F. *The First Hundred Years: A History of the Mennonite Church in Adams County, Indiana, 1838-1935.* Berne, Indiana, 1938.

Steinach, Alderich. *Swiss Colonists in 19th Century America. Reprint of 1889 Edition of Geschichte und Leben der Schweizer Kolonien in den Vereinigten Staaten von Nord-Amerika, with new Introduction in English and four new indexes by Urspeter Schelbert.* Camden, Maine: Picton Press, 1995.

Steinemann, Ernst (ed.). "A List of Eighteenth Century Emigrants from the Canton of Schaffhausen to the American Colonies, 1734-1752," *Pennsylvania-German Folklore Society*, Vol. XVI (Allentown, 1951), pp. 185-196.

St. John's Congregation. *Kirchenbuch (Church Book) for the St. Johannes Gemeinde, Auburn Township, Tuscarawas County, Ohio, 1879-1919.* Sugarcreek, Ohio: St. John's Congregation, 1982.

Stuckey, Walter J. *The Hundredth Anniversary of the Swiss Evangelical and Reformed Church*, New Glarus, Wisconsin, 1958.

Sutter, Leslie E. *Swiss Emigration Agencies: From Shipping Speculators to Travel Agents.* Thesis (Ph.D.), Columbia Pacific University, 1992.

Sutton, David H. *One's Own Hearth Is Like Gold: A History of Helvetia, West Virginia,* Vol. 8, Swiss-American Society Publications, New York, New York: Peter Lang, 1990.

Swiss-German Cultural and Historical Association. *A Study Guide of the Swiss Mennonites Who Came to Kansas in 1874*. Kansas Swiss-German Cultural and Historical Association, 1974.

Switzerland Baptist Church. *History and Directory of the Switzerland Baptist Church of Vevay, Indiana*. Vevay, Indiana: Ladies Aid Society of Switzerland Baptist Church, 1899.

Switzerland of Ohio Vacation Association. *Switzerland of Ohio, Monroe County, Ohio*. Clarington, Ohio: Switzerland of Ohio Vacation Association, 1965.

Theiler, Mrs. Arthur J., "New Glarus, Wisconsin, Translated and Flourishing," in Senn, Alfred (ed.) *The Swiss Record: Yearbook of the Swiss-American Historical Society*, Madison, Wisconsin: Swiss-American Historical Society, Volume I, March 1949, pp. 18-24.

Theiler, Miriam B. *New Glarus' First Hundred Years*. Madison, Wisconsin: Campus Publishing Co., 1946.

Titus, Leo G. "Swiss Emigrants Seek Home in America: Diary Describes Their Impressions of Ohio in 1831," *Historical and Philosophical Society of Ohio Bulletin*, Vol. XIV (July 1956), pp. 167-185.

Todd, Vincent H. *Christoph von Graffenreid's Account of the Founding of New Bern*. Edited with an historical introduction and an English translation in cooperation with Julius Goebel. Raleigh: Edwards & Broughton Printing Co., 1920. Reprint: Spartanburg, South Carolina: The Reprint Co., 1973.

(Video) *A Tour of the Chalet of the Golden Fleece*, 1993, New Glarus Public Library, 319 Second Street, New Glarus, WI 53574.

Tschudy, Millard. *New Glarus' Mirror of Switzerland, 1845-1995*. Monroe, Wisconsin: Monroe Evening Times, 213 Sixth Avenue, New Glarus, Wisconsin, 1995, 7th printing.

Voight, Gilbert Paul. "German and German-Swiss Elements in South Carolina, 1732-52." Columbia: South Carolina, *Bulletin of the University of South Carolina*, No. 113, Sept. 1922.

Von Grüningen, John Paul (ed.). *The Swiss in the United States*. Madison, Wisconsin: Swiss-American Historical Society, 1940.

Waters, Mary Louise. *A Short Historical Sketch of New Bern, North Carolina*. New Bern, North Carolina: Dunn, 1924.

Writer's Program (U.S.). *History of Switzerland County (Indiana)*. Department of Special Collections, Cunningham Memorial Library, Indiana State University, (n.d.).

Wust, Klaus. *Palatines and Switzers for Virginia, 1705-1738: Costly Lessons for Promoters & Emigrants*. Yearbook for German-American Studies 19 (1984): 43-56.

Zollinger, James P. *Sutter: The Man and His Empire*. New York: Oxford University Press, 1939.

## C. Swiss Genealogical Research

Nielson, Paul Anton. *Swiss Genealogical Research: An Introductory Guide*. The Donning Company Publishers, 5041 Admiral Wright Road, Virginia Beach, VA 23462, 1979.

Seuss, Jered H. *Handy Guide to Swiss Genealogical Records*. The Everton Publishers, Inc., P. O. Box 368, Logan, UT 84321, 1978.

Wellauer, Maralyn A. *Tracing Your Swiss Roots*, 2845 N. 72nd Street, Milwaukee, WI 53210, 1979.

## D. Swiss Cookbooks

Benteli Publishers (1990). *Swiss Menu: Gastronomic Souvenirs From Switzerland*. Bern, Switzerland: Benteli Publishers.

Blarer, Ruth von; Geiser, Linda; Prince, Julie. (1991) *Popular Swiss Dishes: What's for Dinner, William Tell?* Linda Geiser, 317 E. 5th Street, New York, NY 10003 ($12.50)

Borer, Eva Marie (1965). *Tante Heidi's Swiss Kitchen*. Nicholas Kaye Ltd., 194-200 Bishopsgate, London, Great Britain, EC 2. ($10.00)

Bührer, Peter. *The New Swiss Cuisine*. Ch-6005, Luzern-St. Niklausen: Medon Verlag, 1991.

Christiansen-Bär, Trudi (1980). *Swiss Cookies*. Edelweiss Publications, 265 Crossroads Square, Salt Lake City, UT 84115. ($12.50, plus postage)

Edelweiss Damenchor (1991). *Our Cookbook: Schweiz*. The Swiss Club, 351 East Gates Street, Columbus, OH 43206 ($6.00, plus $2.00 postage)

Guggenbühl, Helen (1981). *The Swiss Cookery Book: Recipes from All Cantons*. Schweizer Spiegel Verlag, Zürich, Switzerland.

Hazelton, Nika Standen (1984). *The Swiss Cookbook*. Atheneum Press, New York, New York. ($9.00)

Hughes, Hela (1995). *Cooking the Swiss Way*. Minneapolis, Minnesota: Lerner Publications Company.

Kaltenbach, Marianne (1985). *Cooking in Switzerland*. Impressum Verlag AG, Schöneggstrasse 35, CH-8953 Dietikon-Zürich, Switzerland.

Mailloux, Eleanor Fahrner. *Oppis Quel's Vu Helvetia*. The Hütte Restaurant, Box 42, Helvetia, WV 26224, 1969. ($4.50)

Martinet, Jacqueline (1990). *A Little Swiss Cookbook*. San Francisco, California: Chronicle Books. ($7.00).

Mason, Anne (1964). *Swiss Cooking*, London, Great Britain: Andrea Duetsch, Ltd.

Matzinger, Marie, Schiesser, Elda, & Schiesser, Linda. *Swiss Cookery*. Schoco-Laden, New Glarus, WI 53572, 1992. ($4.95)

Monroe (Wisconsin) Swiss Singers and Friends. *Old World Swiss Family Recipes*. Fundcraft Publishing, P. O. Box 340, Collierville, TN 38027.

Nestlé pro Gastronomia Foundation (1992). *Culinary Art and Traditions of Switzerland*. Royale Inter-Continental Industries, 300 N. El Molino Avenue, Pasadena, CA 91101 ($50.00)

New Glarus Chamber of Commerce. *Favorite Recipes from America's Little Switzerland*. New Glarus Tourism & Chamber of Commerce, P. O. Box 713, New Glarus, WI 53574, 48pp., 1995. ($5.99)

Rubin, Cynthia Elyce. *Bread and Chocolate: Culinary Traditions of Switzerland*, 20 West 72nd Street, New York, NY 10023 ($12.00)

San Joaquin Valley Swiss Club. *Kitchen Kubboard Kookbook* (Vol. I & II). 14577 E. French Camp Road, Ripon, CA 95366 ($14.50 each)

Streiff, Doris. *Down on the Farm*. General Publishing & Binding, Inc., R.R. 3, Box 163, Iowa Falls, IA 50126. Vol. 1 (196pp.), Vol. II (314pp.), 1982. ($11.95 each)

Style, Sue (1992). *A Taste of Switzerland*. New York, New York: Hearst Books. ($25.00)

Widmer, Peter (1988). *Culinary Excursions Through Switzerland*. Künzelsau, Germany: Sigloch Edition.

Williams, Anne (1988). *Self-Catering in the Alps*. Christopher Helm (Publishers) Ltd., Imperial House, 21-25 North Street, Bromley, Kent, Great Britain, BRI ISD

# Swiss Consular Representation In North America

## Canada

EMBASSY OF SWITZERLAND
5, AVENUE MARLBOROUGH
OTTAWA, ONTARIO
K1N 8E6, CANADA
    Tel: 613/235-1837
    Fax: 613/563-1394


CONSULATE GENERAL OF SWITZERLAND
1572 AVENUE DR. PENFIELD
MONTREAL, QUEBEC
H3G 1C4, CANADA
    Tel: 514/932-7181/82, 514/932-9757
    Fax: 514/932-9028
    (Consular Jurisdiction: Provinces of Quebec, New Brunswick, Nova Scotia, Prince Edward Island, Newfoundland and the Dependencies of Labrador and Baffin Island)


CONSULATE GENERAL OF SWITZERLAND
154 UNIVERSITY AVENUE, SUITE 601
TORONTO, ONTARIO
M5H 3Y9, CANADA
    Tel: 416/593-5371/73
    Fax: 416/593-5083
    (Consular Jurisdiction: Provinces of Ontario, Manitoba, Saskatchewan)

CONSULATE GENERAL OF SWITZERLAND
WORLD TRADE CENTER
790-999 CANADA PLACE
VANCOUVER, BRITISH COLUMBIA
V6C 3E1, CANADA
    Tel: 604/684-2231
    Fax: 604/684-2806
    (Consular Jurisdiction: Provinces of Alberta and British Columbia, Districts of Franklin, Keewatin, and MacKenzie, Northwest and Yukon Territories)

## UNITED STATES

EMBASSY OF SWITZERLAND
2900 CATHEDRAL AVENUE, N.W.
WASHINGTON, DC 20008-3499
    Tel: 202/745-7900
    Fax: 202/387-2564
    (Consular Jurisdiction: District of Columbia, Delaware, Kentucky, Maryland, Virginia, West Virginia, and U.S. possessions where Switzerland has no representative)

CONSULATE GENERAL OF SWITZERLAND
1275 PEACHTREE STREET, N.E.
SUITE 425
ATLANTA, GA 30309-3555
    Tel: 404/870-2000
    Fax: 404/870-2011
    (Consular Jurisdiction: Alabama, Florida, Georgia, Mississippi, North Carolina, and Tennessee)

CONSULATE GENERAL OF SWITZERLAND
OLYMPIA CENTER, SUITE 2301
737 NORTH MICHIGAN AVENUE
CHICAGO, IL 60611
    Tel: 312/915-0061
    Fax: 312/915-0388
    (Consular Jurisdiction: Illinois, Indiana, Iowa, Michigan, Minnesota, Missouri, Nebraska, North Dakota, South Dakota, Ohio, Wisconsin, Wyoming)

CONSULATE GENERAL OF SWITZERLAND
WELLS FARGO PLAZA
1000 LOUISIANA, SUITE 5670
HOUSTON, TX 77002-5013
    Tel: 713/650-0000
    Fax: 713/650-1321
    (Consular Jurisdiction: Arkansas, Colorado, Kansas, Louisiana, Oklahoma, New Mexico, Texas and British Cayman Islands)


CONSULATE GENERAL OF SWITZERLAND
11766 WILSHIRE BOULEVARD
SUITE 1400
LOS ANGELES, CA 90025
    Tel: 310/575-1145
    Fax: 310/575-1982
    (Consular Jurisdiction: The counties of Southern California, Zips: 90000-93500, and the State of Arizona)


CONSULATE GENERAL OF SWITZERLAND
ROLEX BUILDING, 8TH FLOOR
665 FIFTH AVENUE
NEW YORK, NY 10022-6981
    Tel: 212/758-2560
    Fax: 212/207-8024
    (Consular Jurisdiction: Connecticut, Maine, Massachusetts, New Hampshire, New Jersey, New York, Pennsylvania, Rhode Island, Vermont, Puerto Rico and the U.S. Virgin Islands)


CONSULATE GENERAL OF SWITZERLAND
456 MONTGOMERY STREET
SUITE 1500
SAN FRANCISCO, CA 94104-1233
    Tel: 415/788-2272
    Fax: 415/788-1402
    (Consular Jurisdiction: The counties of Northern California, Zips: over 93501, Alaska, Idaho, Montana, Nevada, Oregon, Utah, Washington and Hawaii)

# SWITZERLAND TOURISM OFFICES IN NORTH AMERICA

(FORMERLY: SWISS NATIONAL TOURIST OFFICE)

## MAIN OFFICE

TOEDISTRASSE 7
CH - 8027 ZÜRICH
SWITZERLAND
    Tel: +41 (0) 1 288 11 11
    Fax: +41 (0) 1 288 1205
    E-mail: Postoffice@Switzerlandtourism.CH
    Internet: http://www.switzerlandtourism.com

## NEW YORK

SWISS CENTER
608 FIFTH AVENUE
NEW YORK, NY 10020-2303
    Tel: 212/757-5944
    Fax: 212/262-6116
    E-mail: STNewYork@Switzerlandtourism.com
    Internet: http://www.switzerlandtourism.com

## LOS ANGELES

222 NORTH SEPULVEDA BOULEVARD, SUITE 1570
EL SEGUNDO, CA 90245
    Tel: 310/640-8900
    Fax: 310/335-5982
    Internet: http://www.switzerlandtourism.com

**CHICAGO**

150 NORTH MICHIGAN AVENUE, SUITE 2930
CHICAGO, IL 60601
    Tel: 312/332-9900
    Fax: 312/630-5848
    Internet: http://www.switzerlandtourism.com

**TORONTO**

926 THE EAST MALL
ETOBICOKE, ONT M9B 6K1
    Tel: 416/695-2090
    Fax: 416/695-2774
    Internet: http://www.switzerlandtourism.com

# SWISS-AMERICAN HISTORICAL SOCIETY

## WASHINGTON, D.C.

Founded in 1927 in Chicago and reactivated in 1964 by Lukas F. Burckhardt and the late Heinz K. Meier, the SAHS unites people interested in the involvement of Swiss and their descendants in American life, in aspects of Swiss American relations, and in Swiss history.

As its name suggests, the Society's activities pertain mainly to Swiss American history. The SAHS promotes historical and genealogical research involving Swiss immigrants. It published Paul Anthon Nielson, *Swiss Genealogical Research: An Introductory Guide* (1979), a valuable tool for those who are researching their family history. It also distributes the guide to *Swiss Festivals in North America* (1995, 1999), prepared by Donald Tritt. The SAHS Publications series, edited by Leo Schelbert, covers topics of Swiss-American interest. Recent titles include: Hedwig Rappolt, ed. and transl., *An American Apprenticeship. The Letters of Emil Frey 1860-1864* (1986); David H. Sutton, *One's Own Hearth Is Like Gold: A History of Helvetia, West Virginia* (1990), and Laura R. Villiger, *Mari Sandoz. A Study in Post-Colonial Discourse* (1994), and Gary K. Pranger, *Philip Schaff, Immigrant Theologian* (1997).

Yet the interests of the SAHS reach beyond history to the broader implications of the ties between the United States and Switzerland. Articles in the *SAHS Review* and papers presented at the Society's annual meetings cover topics such as "Bern, Switzerland, a Medieval City Today" (E. Schmocker); "Benjamin Franklin and Heinrich Zschokke" (D.H. Crosby); "Bombing the Sister Republic: The United States and Switzerland During World War II" (J.H. Hutson); "The Crisis of Switzerland at the Threshold of the European Union" (H.D. Page).

With members mainly in the United States, Canada, and Switzerland, the SAHS fosters contacts on both sides of the Atlantic and serves as a link between Swiss Americans, Swiss, and Americans in an effort to promote cultural awareness and mutual understanding.

Membership is open to all. Members receive the *SAHS Review* three times per year as well as a copy of books published by the Society. The SAHS holds an annual meeting in early October and organizes occasional regional meetings. All work is done on a voluntary basis in order to promote the Society's goals.

## MEMBERSHIP APPLICATION

Name: _____ Date: _____

Street: _____

City, State, Zip: _____

Signature: _____

**Dues are:**
- $ 15.00 for Students
- $ 30.00 for Individuals
- $ 45.00 for Institutions
- $350.00 for Life Members

Mail check, payable to SAHS, to:
Prof. Erdmann Schmocker
6440 N. Bosworth Ave.
Chicago, IL 60626

# TELL US!
## WHAT HAVE WE FORGOTTEN?

Is there a favorite Swiss festival of yours not included here? Please let us know about other festivals we should include in the next edition.

Festival: _____

Town: _____

Province/State: _____

Postal/Zip Code: _____

Telephone: _____


What other features would you like to see in the next edition of this book? We thank you for your suggestions!

# PUBLICATIONS ORDER FORM

(Please copy pages 183 and 184 to place an order.)

1. *Swiss Genealogical Research*; by Paul Anton Nielson, Donning Press, Virginia Beach, Norfolk, VA, 1979; 85 pages .................................. $5.00

2. *The United States and Switzerland: Aspects of an Enmeshment*; Yearbook of German American Studies 1990; Vol. 25; edited by Leo Schelbert; University of Kansas, Lawrence, KS; 279 pages ...... $15.00

3. *Mari Sandoz; A Study in Post-Colonial Discourse*; by Laura R. Villiger; Peter Lang Verlag; New York, NY, 1994; 215 pages .............................. $15.00

4. *An American Apprenticeship: The Letters of Emil Frey 1860-1865*; edited and translated by Hedwig Rappolt; Peter Lang Verlag, New York, NY, 1986; 227 pages ..................................... $15.00

5. *The Dorlikon Emigrants*; by Konrad Basler; Peter Lang Verlag, New York, NY, 1996; 75 pages ......... $10.00

6. *With a Horse Called George Along the Oregon Trail*; by Hafis Bertschinger, Idaho State University Press; Pocatello, ID, 1996; illustrated; 191 pages .... $12.50

7. *Mennonites in Transition: From Switzerland to America*; edited by Andrea Boldt, Werner Enninger, Delbert Gratz; Masthof Press, Morgantown, PA, 1997; illustrated; 138 pages ..................... $15.00

(continued on next page)

8. ***The Sister Republics: Switzerland and the United States from 1776 to the Present***; by James Hutson; Library of Congress, Washington, DC, 1991; illustrated; 77 pages; revised 2nd edition ............... $10.00

9. ***Philip Schaff; 1819-1893; Portrait of an Immigrant Theologian***; by Gary K. Pranger; Peter Lang Verlag, New York, NY, 1997; 305 pages ........... $15.00

10. ***Helvetica Americana***; US map with a selection of Swiss names of related settlements, 24" x 24"; compiled by Erdmann Schmocker; Chicago, IL, 1991; ready for framing .................. $20.00

11. Souvenir T-Shirts; collectors' item **"700 Years Switzerland" 1291-1991** with US/Swiss logo, sizes M, XL .................................. $5.00

12. **"150 Years New Glarus. Wisconsin 1995**; cacheted envelope with special cancel .................... $2.00

13. **"100 Year Bern, Kansas,"** 1987, Postcard with special cancel ................................ $2.00

14. **Lapel Pins**, Swiss-American Flag ................. $2.50

Name: _____

Address: _____

_____

*Please enclose 10% for postage and handling (minimum of 33¢).*

**Make checks payable and send orders to:**
Swiss-American Historical Society
6440 No. Bosworth Avenue
Chicago, IL 60626

# INDEX TO EVENTS BY MONTH

## JANUARY

*3rd week:*
　　Kaffeeklatsch, New York City
*4th week:*
　　Swiss Banquet & Ball, New York City

## FEBRUARY

*2nd week:*
　　Fasnacht, Helvetia, WV
*3rd week:*
　　Kaffeeklatsch, New York City
*(Easter Time)*
　　Heimatabig, Bethesda, MD

## MARCH

*3rd week:*
　　Swiss Theater Evening, Toronto, Ontario
　　Kaffeeklatsch, New York City
*4th week:*
　　Swiss Ski Cup, Vail, CO

## APRIL

*2nd week:*
　　Swiss Jass Championship, New York City
*3rd week:*
　　Kaffeeklatsch, New York City

## May

*1st week:*
 Swiss Benefit Dinner, New York City
*3rd week:*
 Polkafest, New Glarus, WI
 Kaffeeklatsch, New York City
*4th week:*
 Spring Schwingfest, Newark, CA

## June

*1st week:*
 Swiss Picnic, Toledo, OH
*2nd week:*
 Schweitzerfest, Highland, IL
*3rd week:*
 Pacific Coast Swiss Singing & Yodeling Festival, Salt Lake City, UT
*4th week:*
 North American Swiss Singing Festival, Edmonton, Alberta
 Heidi Festival & Little Switzerland Festival, New Glarus, WI

## July

*3rd week:*
 Swiss Sunday, Alma, WI
 Kaffeeklatsch, New York City
*4th week:*
 Swiss Days, Berne, IN
 Swiss Reunion & Celebration, Gruetli-Laager, TN

## AUGUST

*1st week:*
    Fall Schwingfest, Tacoma, WA
    Portland Schwingfest, Portland, OR
    First of August, Clarksburg, NJ
    First of August, Chicago, IL
    First of August, Vail, CO
    First of August, Sabastopol, CA
    First of August, Palo Alto, CA
    First of August, Newark, CA
    First of August, Rockford, MN
    Volksfest, New Glarus, WI
    Swiss Fair, Whittier, CA
    National Day of Celebration, Rockwood, Ontario
    Berne Swissfest, Berne, MN
    Swiss National Day Celebration, New York City
    Swiss Week & Swissfair, Spartanburg, SC

*3rd week:*
    Swiss Wine Festival, Vevay, IN
    New Schwanden Swiss Families Reunion & Picnic,
        Brooklyn, MN

*4th week:*
    Fall Schwingfest, Newark, CA
    Schwingest & Musikfest, Ripon, CA


## SEPTEMBER

*1st week:*
    Swiss Days, Midway, UT
    Wilhelm Tell Pageant & Alpine Festival, New Glarus, WI

*2nd week:*
    Oktoberfest, Mt. Angel, OR
    Swiss Week, Chicago, IL

*3rd week:*
    Green County Cheese Days & Swiss Folk Fair, Monroe, WI
    Kaffeeklatsch, New York City

## October

*1st week:*
 Ohio Swiss Festival, Sugarcreek, OH
*2nd week:*
 Octoberfest, New Glarus, WI
 Schützenfest, Coquitlam, British Columbia
*3rd week:*
 Kaffeeklatsch, New York City

## November

*1st week:*
 Swiss Fest, Monroe, WI
*2nd week:*
 Metzgete, Palo Alta, CA
*3rd week:*
 Kaffeeklatsch, New York City

## December

*1st week:*
 Swiss Club Dinner & Concert, Columbus, OH
 Swiss Christmas Library Dinner, Highland, IL
 Weihnachts Feier, Glenwood Springs, CO
 Christkindlmarkt, Monroe, WI
 Deutscher Weihnachtsgottesdienst, Monroe, WI

# Roberts European Imports
## New Glarus' Largest Importer!

We specialize in Swiss imports. Many of our items are imported directly from artists and craftsmen, and are found in America exclusively at Roberts European Imports – the Swiss Store in the USA!

- Fondue Pans, Burners & Supplies
- Raclette Grills
- Swiss Langenthal Porcelain China
- Swiss Milking Jackets
- Embroidered Herdmans shirts
- Embroidered hiking boots and walking shoes from Davos
- Scarves & Handkerchiefs with Edelweiss and/or Folklore designs in Silk or Cotton
- Swiss Bells from Appenzell
- Swiss Design Napkins & Placemats
- Swiss Flags and Canton Shields
- Swiss Scene Calendars – printed or fabric
- Swiss Scene Note Cards
- Victorinox Swiss Army Knives
- Swiss Bell Door Chimes
- Music Boxes
- Swiss Watches and Cuckoo Clocks
- Bratzeli Irons (Brezeleisen)
- Pure Gold Bar Necklaces
- Swiss Music – Yodel - Laendler - Oergeli or Combination. CD's or Cassettes

Fondue Supplies

Langenthal China – We're the exclusive USA Importer!

Milking Jackets

Visit our web site:
**www.shopswiss.com**
Send email to:
**robertsj@shopswiss.com**

Ask for a copy of our free catalog.
*Wholesale available to qualified buyers.*

102 Fifth Avenue, New Glarus, WI 53574
(608) 527-2517 • Fax (608) 527-2107
(800) 968-2517

Bratzeli Irons (Brezeleisen)

*Enjoy a European Vacation right here at home.*

Visit New Glarus, Wisconsin—America's "Little Switzerland"

## New Glarus Hotel Restaurant

Experience the historic New Glarus Hotel, in the center of America's Little Switzerland! Built by Swiss immigrants in 1853, the Hotel has long been a landmark known for its fine Swiss cuisine.

Enjoy a luncheon or dinner, with authentic Swiss food and atmosphere. Dine and dance every Friday and Saturday night year round, to the music of the famous Roger Bright Polka Band. Special group and bus menus available. Please call for information at (800) 727-9477 or (608) 527-5244.

New Glarus Hotel, 100-6th Avenue, New Glarus, WI 53574

web site: www.newglarushotel.com    email: hotel@newglarushotel.com

## Chalet Landhaus Inn

The Chalet Landhaus Inn is built in traditional Swiss style–with a perfect blend of modern convenience and old-fashioned Swiss decor—to give you a taste of Switzerland close to home. Group rates available. For information and reservations, please call (800) 944-1716 or (608) 527-5234.

Chalet Landhaus Inn, 801 Highway 69, New Glarus, WI 53574

web site: www.chaletlandhaus.com    email: info@chaletlandhaus.com

New Glarus, settled by Swiss immigrants in 1845, proudly maintains it's Swiss heritage. The annual Swiss festivals and music, Swiss architecture, flowers, flowerboxes, and cuisine, present a European experience—right at home. New Glarus has many unique shops, two historical museums, and is headquarters of the popular Sugar River Bike Trail.

And it's only a short drive from Monroe, Spring Green, Mt. Horeb, Mineral Point, and favorite Wisconsin attractions—the House on the Rock, The Fireside Dinner Theatre, Casinos. It's the perfect location for your extended vacation!

# Catorex Swiss Watch

*High Quality since 1858*

Guarantee worldwide

Pocket & Pendant Watches

## Our other Products

*Folklore Style (Edelweiss, Enzian etc.)*

**Fashion Jewelry**
**Paper Napkins**
**Caps**
**Handkerchiefs**
**Doilies**
**Aprons**
**Kitchen Coordinates**
**Glarner Scarf's**
**Tervis Tumblers**
**Souvenir Spoons**
**Patches Emblems**
**Music Boxes**

Wrist Watches

Ask for brochures

# ALIMPEX TRADE, INC.

7820 Craighurst Loop   New Port Richey, FL 34655
Phone/Fax  813 375 5103   E-mail: alimpex@gte.net

**Die besten Videos und Musik von der Schweiz**

Made for North America

Prices lower than in Switzerland !

Please write or call for free list.
Bitte schreiben oder anrufen für gratis Liste.

**MARKUS VIDEO**
P.O. Box 277, Islington,
Ont., Canada M9A 4X2
1-800-567-7152
Fax: 1-416-239-2069

# What's for Dinner, William Tell ?

A Swiss cookbook in English

To order, call or write:

Linda Geiser
317 East 5th Street
New York, N.Y. 10003
Tel & Fax 212 673 5422

($15, postpaid)

## GERMAN SPEAKING RESEARCH BOOKS

**1345. Pennsylvania German Pioneers: The original Lists of Arrivals in the Port of Philadelphia 1727 to 1808.** Vol. I $65.00; Vol. II $70.00; Vol. III $60.00; all 3 vols. $175.00

**1639. Emigrants from Baden and Württemberg in the 18$^{th}$ century Vol. 1: Baden Durlach and vicinity.** $49.50

**1797. Emigrants from Baden and Württemberg in the 19$^{th}$ century Vol. 1: The Enzkreis.** $45.00

**1416. 18$^{th}$ Century Emigrants from the Northern Alsace to America.** $49.50

**1630. Swiss Surnames: A complete Register.** 3 vol. set $149.50

**1490. Bibliography of Swiss Genealogies.** $59.50

**1607. Swiss Colonists in 19$^{th}$ century America.** $49.50

**1530. America Experienced: 18$^{th}$ and 19$^{th}$ Century Accounts of Swiss Immigrants to the US.** $29.50

**1600. An American Apprenticeship: The letters of Emil Frey 1860-1865.** $17.50

Call or write for free catalog with full descriptions on these books as well as all others available from Picton Press.

PICTON PRESS

Order any of the above books from **Picton Press**, PO Box 250, Rockport, ME 04856-0250 or call (207) 236-6565 Shipping & handling $4.00 for 1 book; $2.00 for each additional book

## *THE SWISS CONNECTION*
A Genealogical and Cultural Newsletter

*The Swiss Connection* is published quarterly for Americans of Swiss descent. Queries are free to subscribers. Back issues are still available. We are a clearinghouse for Swiss genealogical information. Subscription rate for one year: Domestic **$12.** Foreign **$20.**

Maralyn A. Wellauer, Editor
**2845 North 72nd Street, Milwaukee, WI 53210**
**Fax**: 414.778.2109; **E-mail**: swissmis@interserv.com
Visit our **website** at: http://www.feefhs.org/ch/tsc/frg-tsc.html

---

GEORGE & URSULA ALTHER

## A TOUCH OF SWITZERLAND
Scherenschnitte & Woodcarvings
Landlermusic & Souvenirs

*Ask for our catalog*

P.O. Box 4300
Auburn, CA 95604-4300

Phone & Fax
530-887-9342

## A S N
### Services for expariates

## MAKING LIFE JUST A LITTLE EASIER

**Swiss Private Pension**

✓ Guaranteed interest rate
✓ Guaranteed risk benefits
✓ Swiss rock solid asset protection with the best Swiss Insurance Companies

**Investment**

✓ Define your own investment profile with us
✓ select the best solution for your needs

**ASN, Advisory Services Network AG**
Seestrasse 353, CH-8038 Zürich-Wollishofen
Tel: (41) 1 / 284 37 86    Fax: (41) 1 / 284 37 46
Internet: http://www.asn.ch

**ASN**
ADVISORY SERVICES NETWORK

Services for expariates

presents:

## World-Wide Private Medical Insurance

Do you require a guarantee of medical insurance on a world-wide, life-long basis?

**Comprehensive Swiss-style benefits include:**

- ✓ private medical treatment
- ✓ world-wide free choice of doctor, hospital and clinic
- ✓ life-long guaranteed cover
- ✓ multilingual 24-hour alarm line

**ASN, Advisory Services Network AG**
Seestrasse 353, CH-8038 Zürich-Wollishofen
Tel: (41) 1 / 284 37 86    Fax: (41) 1 / 284 37 46
Internet: http://www.asn.ch

# ABOUT THE AUTHOR

Donald G. Tritt, born in Ohio of Swiss ancestry, is professor emeritus of psychology at Denison University, Granville, Ohio. He has a B.S. degree from The Ohio State University and a Ph.D. degree from the University of Chicago. In addition to being a member of the board of trustees of the Columbus, Ohio, Grütli Verein and chairing its history and genealogy committee, he serves as a member of the board of trustees of the Columbus Swiss Home Association. Since 1990, he has served as a member of the national advisory board of the Swiss-American Historical Society and, in 1998, was elected First Vice-President of the Society.